INTO THE STORY

Language in Action Through Drama

Carole Miller and Juliana Saxton

HEINEMANN
Portsmouth, NH

Heinemann

361 Hanover Street
Portsmouth, NH 03801–3912
www.heinemann.com

Offices and agents throughout the world

The author and publisher wish to thank those who have generously given permission to reprint borrowed material:

Excerpts from *The Pumpkin Blanket* written and illustrated by Deborah Turney Zagwÿn. Copyright © 1995 by Deborah Turney Zagwÿn. Reprinted by permission of Fitzhenry & Whiteside.

Excerpts from *Peter and the Wolf* retold and illustrated by Michele Lemieux. Text and illustration copyright © 1991 by Michele Lemieux. Reprinted by permission of the author.

Excerpts from *The Very Best of Friends*. Text Copyright © 1989 by Margaret Wild. Reprinted by permission of Harcourt, Inc.

Excerpts from *The Tunnell* by Anthony Browne. Text Copyright © 1989 by Anthony Browne. Reprinted by permission of Walker Books Ltd.

Excerpts from *The Polar Express* by Chris Van Allsburg. Text Copyright © 1985 by Chris Van Allsburg. Reprinted by permission of Houghton Mifflin Company. All rights reserved.

Excerpts from *The Werewolf Knight* by Jenny Wagner, published in 1995. Reprinted by permission of Random House Australia.

Illustration by Karen Reczuch from *The Dust Bowl* by David Booth. Text copyright © 1996 by David Booth. Reprinted by permission of Kids Can Press Ltd., Toronto.

Excerpts from *Josepha: A Prairie Boy's Story* by Jim McGugan. Text copyright © 1994 by Jim McGugan. Illustration copyright © 1994 by Murray Kimber. Reprinted by permission of Red Deer Press.

Excerpts from *Only Opal: The Diary of a Young Girl* by Jane Boulton. Text Copyright © 1994 by Jane Boulton. Illustration Copyright © 1994 by Barbara Cooney. Reprinted by permission of the author.

Adaptation of *Opal: The Journey of an Understanding Heart* by Jane Boulton. Text Copyright © 1995 by Jane Boulton. Used with permission of the author.

Excerpts from *Letting Swift River Go* by Jane Yolen. Text Copyright © 1992 by Jane Yolen. Illustrations Copyright © 1992 by Barbara Cooney. Reprinted by permission of Little, Brown and Company, Inc.

Library of Congress Cataloging-in-Publication Data
Miller, Carole S.
    Into the story : language in action through drama / Carole Miller, Juliana Saxton.
      p. cm.
    Includes bibliographical references and index.
    ISBN 0-325-00628-8 (alk. paper)
    1. Language arts (Elementary). 2. Drama in education. 3. English language—Study and teaching (Elementary)—Activity programs. I. Saxton, Juliana, 1933–
II. Title.

LB1575.8.M55 2004
372.6—dc22   2003020231

Editor: Lisa A. Barnett
Production coordinator: Elizabeth Valway
Production service: Denise A. Botelho
Cover art and conceptual work: Jenny Lora Miller
Cover design: Joni Doherty
Composition: Publishers' Design and Production Service, Inc.
Manufacturing: Steve Bernier

Printed in the United States of America on acid-free paper
T & C Digital

Literacy . . . is language *in action*. It makes things happen, it is a means of transforming your world, it is the essential that joins cause and effect in human affairs.
—JONOTHAN NEELANDS, 2000

Our species thinks in metaphors and learns through stories.
—MARY CATHERINE BATESON, 1994

Drama is the act of crossing into the world of story. . . . Storying provides students with a natural human process for finding essential meanings in the life experiences of themselves and others.
—DAVID BOOTH, 1995

Drama is a medium through which children are helped to actively explore the structure and meaning of narratives individually, in groups, and as a whole class. . . . Drama moves children closer to the fiction and helps them to find forms through which to communicate their personal and collective responses.
—PATRICE BALDWIN, 1998

Acknowledgments

The story drama structure for *Peter and the Wolf* is based on the work of Jane Holden, and we are extremely grateful to her for giving us permission to use her ideas; they are integral to the structure. We wish to thank Robyn Cusworth and Jenny Simons for introducing us to *The Werewolf Knight*, for the richness of their ideas and kind permission to build on their work. Thank you to Jacqui Coulson for her wonderful ideas about *The Dust Bowl* and *The Pumpkin Blanket* and to Linda Laidlaw for her contributions to the story drama structure based on *Josepha: a prairie boy's story*. Barbara Menzies introduced us to *Letting Swift River Go* and shared her ideas with us; Mary Bomhof gave us the optional strategy for *The Tunnel*. We'd like to thank Pat Miller of Storyline Books, Victoria, British Columbia, and Lara Riecken, youth librarian, Esquimalt Branch, Greater Victoria Public Library, for recognizing some great sources for drama. Sarah Harvey of the University of Victoria Bookstore, a recently published author, knows the strains and delights of book searches better than most and always responded cheerfully to our plaintive cries for help.

We are extremely grateful to the teachers and students of Victoria, Saanich, and Sooke School Districts, who have invited us into their schools and piloted much of the material that appears in this book. Without their responses, we would not be so confident that the structures do work. Jon Champion and Alison Froom gave us permission to use their words; they add to the authenticity of our research and we thank them.

Cris Warner and her students at Ohio State University have been willing and enthusiastic testers of the structures and we thank them for their contributions. Our own students over the years have given so much to the development of the structures. They took risks both in our classes and in their practica classrooms. They never failed to tell us what worked and what didn't; they have allowed us to use their commentaries and pointed us to new literature and new ideas. The structures they have devised for themselves based on our models deserve their own publication.

There are a number of colleagues and master teachers whose work and writing have informed our own. Their examples of theory and practice have had significant influence on the development and implementation of these story drama structures: Gavin Bolton, David Booth, Norah Morgan, Jonothan Neelands, and Cecily O'Neill. In the field of literacy education, Alison Preece has been friend, colleague, and thoughtful critic, as has Jo O'Mara. Mary Pratt Cooney encouraged us by sharing her stories of teaching the structures. In all honesty, none of this work would have been possible without a lot of help from our friends whose names and work you will find in the bibliography.

The fine editorial eye of Margaret Burke has been an invaluable constrainer of our worst excesses. Lisa Barnett of Heinemann has remained a steady helmswoman through thick and thin.

Contents

For Harvey, Jill, Joseph, Margaret, and Barbara
They know why

Foreword

It works.

I've seen it work—

> ... with classes of six year olds; with students in grade three, and five, and high school; with young adults nervous in a second language; with student teachers; with the confident; with the cautious.
>
> ... and I've been captivated, moved, and *surprised*, at the responses generated, at the "largeness" of what is unleashed, at the sense of satisfaction and accomplishment that lingers after. At what the dramas make possible.

This works.

The approaches offered here provide tools and techniques for richly connecting with texts judiciously chosen to be worth such investment. Wise in the ways of the classroom, Miller and Saxton have created a resource that makes the power and craft of process drama accessible and transparent. More than that, they've made it inviting, unintimidating, and enticingly available to those who may never have tried such strategies before, or even have imagined that they could. It's impossible to observe these lessons in action without recognizing the quality of the experiences they enable.

As a language arts educator with a keen interest but no formal background in drama, I've had many opportunities over the past five years to observe firsthand the impact and the evolution of these drama frames. I've jumped at invitations to sit in and watch as classes from local elementary schools—most with no previous exposure to drama—have visited our campus to participate in these lessons. I've talked with accompanying parents, as they, leaning forward in their seats, watched their child in role, transformed. Intrigued and impressed, I've tracked and analyzed the range and variety of the language the students use and are exposed to as these dramas unfold. I've been present as teachers new in the profession, and others experienced but new to drama, have tried these lessons out. And I've seen them moved and surprised, just as I have been, by what children, alive inside these dramas, reveal they understand, feel, and know.

Drama has long been acknowledged as a compelling medium for learning. The "let's pretend" impulse at its heart is childhood's own. Spontaneously and naturally, children slip in and out of roles and scenarios of their own imagining, taking on and trying out new identities and testing themselves in situations and settings they concoct, control, and complicate. "Making believe," they expand and explore who they might be and become, how they might be, and what they might do. They play with, and play out, options, alternatives, possibilities, impossibilities. And in the doing of it, in the being of it, they learn lessons about themselves and the world we could not teach them otherwise. To observe children engaged in such play is to observe an intensity of attention, an absorption, and an integrity of ownership that is striking testimony to its value.

Tapping into this same impulse, these story dramas invite students to be "players," and in the enactment and unfolding of these lessons, a similar intensity, focus, and immediacy is evident. Convincingly so. *Things matter. Something must be done. Decisions must be made. Now. Actions have consequences. Positions need defending. Nothing is simple. All are implicated. And who is to act, if not us?*

What results is much more than mere "response." Scaffolded by the story, the drama draws all in. The strategies so carefully linked in these lessons allow participants to come together, to shape, share, and reshape their understandings; to explore directly and render real the issues, dilemmas, dangers, and delights inherent in the narratives presented. It's powerful pedagogy. It's literacy at its most robust. It's learning that stretches.

This is a book designed for teachers who conceptualize learning as active interpretation, as shared construction, as composition rather than replication. It's for teachers who reject and rail against limitingly functional models of literacy. It's for teachers who respect and recognize the capacity of learners to engage profoundly, to care, to believe, and to invest. It's for teachers who seek out ways to make the learning matter, the thinking deep. At the same time, it's written by two educators who understand from the inside the realities and pressures teachers confront daily: the dauntingly overcrowded curriculum, the increasing constraint of accountability, escalating expectations, public scrutiny, inevitable time limitations. There are risks in trying something new. For many, attractive though it might be, drama represents risk. Knowing this, and the legitimate anxieties and questions of those who wish to try but have not been trained to be drama teachers, the authors provide foundation and structure. While never patronizing, they give clear and comprehensive guidance with the why and the how of the methods made explicit at every stage. The lessons are completely outlined; close attention to practical detail makes plain how thoroughly each has been tested and refined. Revision of the frameworks has been ongoing and responsive; each has been implemented many times with different groups, of different ages, in different settings. Miller and Saxton are demanding critics of their own work, ever sensitive to what needs to be clarified, what could be sharpened, better scaffolded, opened up. And, although designed so as to be readily implemented by those new to the pedagogy of drama, the standards of the craft are never compromised. Perhaps that is one of the reasons this book means so much to me; it's the inherent respect for the discipline that is conveyed, and for the professionalism and capabilities of educators striving to make that discipline their own.

Alison Preece, Ph.D.
Pender Island, British Columbia

CHAPTER ONE

Falling into the Stories

When we are in drama, it is like walking in the pages of a book.
The words do not just lie there; they come alive and walk with us.
That makes me want to stay in the drama because I don't want to
leave the words behind.

(BEATRICE, CITED IN WARNER 1997)

Over thirty years ago, James Moffett (1968) recognized that drama was a supremely effective way to "walk in the pages of a book." David Booth (1994), building on Moffett's work, has made drama accessible to thousands of teachers and students around the world through his work with story drama. While he uses many different kinds of stories, children's picture books are central to his drama practice; he calls them "his friends." For teachers, picture books are familiar, accessible, and safe; for students, these books can become, through drama, entries into the world of their own narratives. Moffett's early work in conveying the importance of speaking and listening as basic to developing the skills of reading and writing has been supported most recently through the longitudinal studies of the impact of the arts on learning (see Deasy 2002). Drama as a medium for literacy is becoming recognized worldwide (Ackroyd 2000; Baldwin 1998; Cusworth and Simons 1997; O'Toole 2002).

Today it is not uncommon to find drama or drama activities suggested as curriculum pedagogy for a variety of subject areas or as an independent subject. While drama may have become an accepted means of integrating active learning experiences, the majority of elementary and middle school teachers have had few opportunities for professional development. Many view it as lying outside their fields of expertise and beyond their capabilities. How then can we expect teachers to become aware of the power of drama as a learning integrator, let alone as an art form? How, without any experience or discipline-based language, can teachers access resources and/or understand how to use the examples of drama practice? And when will they find the time for any of this?

For a number of years, we have been capitalizing on the friendliness of picture books by piloting, with students and their teachers, a series of detailed drama lessons that we call story drama structures. According to Taylor (2000), in story drama the action develops as participants work through or solve the problems and issues in the story without having to act out the story or remember their lines. Our primary focus was to use these story drama structures to open teachers to the possibilities of drama as a classroom methodology; it was their students' enthusiastic responses that validated the process.

Drama and Three-Dimensional Literacy

We read castle, dragon, and knight stories; kids went on the Internet and found castle information. They made swords, helmets, and daggers in art, drew a million castles, and wrote great stories! Elaine, who was a really struggling grade-two reader, has been practicing reading the book, and to her delight, she can! (Teacher, grade 1/2)

The teachers we have worked with see drama as a "fun" activity; they also recognize immediately the power of the art form for teaching multiple literacies. As Lee and Fradd (1998) point out, "Literacy development involves abilities well beyond being able to speak, listen, read and write. . . . It involves learning to observe, predict, analyze, summarize and present information in a variety of formats" (14). Drama offers learners a direct means of uncovering curriculum, providing opportunities for them to interpret and to make sense of their worlds.

When students engage holistically, affectively, and cognitively with the meanings offered in a story, they develop new ways of seeing the content at both the interpersonal and the intrapersonal levels (Gardner 1983). It is their physical engagement offered through the medium of drama—the taking on of a role in imagined situations—that connects and mediates affective and cognitive understandings and deepens students' recognition of who they are in relation to others in a community of learners.

There are three foundational elements to theater practice: community, empathy, and shared meaning. The very nature of dramatic engagement implies action—the basis of experiential learning (think of the words we use: *acts, actors, acting*). We know from the research that feelings play a vital role in effective thinking and decision making (Damasio 1994; 1999). Schools are communities where learning takes place in a social context. Drama is a social art form that requires an *other* to have *affect* and *effect*. The playing out and negotiation of meaning is what lies at the heart of dramatic engagement. In drama, "the power of the work . . . not only permit[s] but also demand[s] that we discover other versions of ourselves in the roles

The imagined worlds, the atmosphere, the encounters with new characters and situations, the teasing out of feelings and concerns about who we are and who we are becoming offer children such a powerful, engaging opportunity not just to learn what language is but to learn what it does; how it shapes our identities, defines our worlds, joins us together and yet also divides us. (Neelands 2000, vi)

we play or watch other actors playing" (O'Neill 1991, 23). Together we discover why things are the way they are and are able to explore possibilities for change.

Booth and Barton (2000) tell us that when students use drama to explore the themes and issues of a story, "they begin to draw upon their own experiences and to see story incidents from the viewpoint of themselves and others" (81). In a number of structures, students are required to change roles and this shift in perspective provides opportunities for them to evaluate their own actions and words from a different point of view. In this way, students have opportunities to develop that sense of social responsibility that Haseman (2003) sees as an integral learning outcome.

While not every story, poem, play, novel, or article should be explored through drama, experiences *in* drama promote a literacy that is three-dimensional. Drama makes it possible for students to represent their understandings in a variety of ways that are not available through more traditional methodologies. And when students sit down to read or write, they bring those internalized drama experiences to the little black marks on the page. They hear the different voices; they sense the different moods; they place themselves in different roles; they experience the landscape in which they find themselves; they feel the dryness of the earth, the sharpness of the dagger, the barb of the wire. They know for themselves and in themselves, through their bodies, the expressions and gestures that authors can only describe in words. At the same time, they are also observers, bringing their own values, attitudes, and perspectives into play (Morgan and Saxton 1998). That is to say, when someone is working in role, they are able to hold both the fictional world and the real world in the mind at the same time. For example, although the magician in *The Werewolf Knight* is plotting his future ascent to the throne, the student recognizes how evil he is really being.

Choosing the Stories

Picture books build connections to learning experiences for students. One of the most important reasons and one of the most neglected, is the delight (aka "fun") in the shared experience of an apparently simple story accompanied by often powerful illustrations. For readers who are turned off by pages of close print, the brevity of text, accessible language, and quality of artwork mitigates against their resistance. There are few words in a picture book but the words chosen hold resonances of metaphor, symbolism, and poetry. They offer models for rich language development and

> *Never has mourning had such a sweet air. I see all the court draped in black and my heart is like a hawk soaring above it all. Soon she will be forced to abandon her black cloaks and will want comfort. And who else to comfort her than he who knows the darkest secret?* (Student's writing in role)

> **Dust Bowl**
>
> What once was gold
> Now is dust
> What was first a yellow ocean
> Is now vast and scorching
> What was once rich black soil
> Now is dust like snow
> Farming is now a
> Slow way to starve
> All hope is lost
> Lonely, cut off from the world
> Ghost town
> The world is a barren
> Dust Bowl
> *(Alison, grade five)*

expand students' awareness of the many genres available to them as writers (Miller 1998). "Good literature gives readers something to care about" (Estes and Vásquez-Levy 2001, 507). For these reasons, many teachers are using picture books with adolescents and pre-adolescents as well as with young children.

"Choosing picture books which lend themselves to drama isn't that simple a thing," Andy Kempe (1997), the English drama educator, cautions. He suggests that we "look for books which seem to have gaps in the story where something must have happened which isn't clearly told; . . . for stories which suggest other stories . . . and stories which show different attitudes of people" (np). The "gaps" make space in which students can explore possibilities, while at the same time having to make those possibilities "fit" into what is already written. Stories with dramatic potential allow us to find other stories that, however different, address the same themes, feelings, and attitudes. Stories are always more interesting when they investigate the ambiguities of human behavior and range of human feelings.

In making our selections, we wanted to choose a range of stories that represented a gender balance. Yet unlike in casting for a play, gender is not an issue. In drama, we are exploring people's attitudes and points of view, and so anyone can play any role; we take on roles against type and against gender all the time. Herein lies the difference between drama and theater as it applies to the classroom, making it a most egalitarian pedagogy.

When we've found a story that appears to be "right," our criteria become a little more specific:

- The language and illustrations are rich and evocative.
- The material in the story expands and/or deepens learning in terms of specific curriculum and/or the "hidden" curriculum (Sautter 1994).
- We feel some personal attachment to the ideas, themes, and the underlying human issues.
- There is something in the story that we know will engage our students.

Each story acts as a lens into the human condition whether it be historical, fantastical, social, or personal. At the beginning of each structure, we note the connections both to the curriculum and to the hidden curriculum and we offer our own key understandings and questions. Of course, you will find your own as you work with the structures.

Creating the Story Drama Structures

When we introduced these structures to our students and teachers in the field and piloted them with our drama colleagues, we received a lot of mixed messages. On the one hand, the highly detailed "recipes" made it possible for inexperienced and generalist teachers to have the confidence to bring drama into their classrooms. On the other, our colleagues felt that we were creating "scripts" for teachers that would negate their creativity and ignore the needs of their individual students. Where was the joy in the exploration of possibilities? These "scripts" were examples of "doing to" students. Where was their ownership? If we provided the lessons, how would teachers ever learn to plan drama for themselves? Valid questions and ones that concerned us, too.

When we present teachers with a drama structure where all the words for the teacher are provided, how do we allow for flexibility, for the teacher's experience and sense of professional autonomy? How can we take a descriptive narrative and transform it into teacher action language "to shape," as Barone (1998) writes, "situations that . . . can result in aesthetic experiences for teacher[s] and [their] students" (1107)? What description will we need in order to clarify what is happening, what needs to happen, and how to make it happen? How do we present the structure on the page so that a teacher can pick it up and work directly and easily from it?

This is an approach that could be described as prescriptive. Our aim was to scaffold the work for novice teachers and teachers new to drama by giving them clear, thorough guidelines that they could try out and have success with, and through which they could develop their own skills. While seasoned drama teachers may enjoy the risks of "leading the way while walking backwards . . . not knowing what lies ahead" (O'Neill 1995, 67), for most of us, particularly if we are new to drama teaching, it's very helpful to have an idea of where we are going and when we will arrive. The structures are intended to be well-mapped journeys rather than resting places (O'Mara 2001). In the five years that we have been developing the template for the structures, teachers have not been resting comfortably but are adapting the structures and activities in all sorts of ways.

Despite colleagues' concerns that these structures will simply be repeated by teachers time after time with no change, they have forgotten that although the content is the same year after year, the classroom contexts are always different and it is this difference that teachers recognize and respond to intuitively. As Holden (1994) points out, "As often as we do the 'same' drama, every drama is different, regardless of whether the same stimulus and/or starting point are used each time. Each drama is created by a particular group of [students], in a particular school, at a particular time" (9).

As tightly structured as the drama is for the teacher, it is actually an open structure for the students, inviting them to become co-creators. For that reason, at the same time that we are "dictating" to the teacher what to say, we rarely include student responses. We only illustrate with a student comment when it may help the teacher to be aware of the kinds of things students *might* say. You will notice that there is quite a lot of "white space" in each structure between the teacher's talk. This space is offered in graphic form to represent students' thinking and/or talking time and to help the teacher slow the pace.

Although there may be an apparent developmental order in the structures, we have noticed that teachers are finding ways to adapt what might on the surface appear to be age-specific. For example, we thought that Of Dark and Wolfish Things would be best suited to an intermediate level in the autumn. Not so! Our colleague who piloted it with her grade 1-2 split class wrote, "What a great unit! And we didn't do it at Halloween; January is just as good! . . . [Although] I don't know really whether the wedding is too hard [for this age group] or if I was having a bad day!" She's right. The wedding is a tricky strategy for younger children because the teacher is not in role along with them and they must make it work by themselves. However, that didn't stop them!

A Powerful Thirst was designed for and piloted with grades five through eight, yet we taught it without adaptation to a mixed group of grades eleven and twelve students participating in a drama festival. While both groups were aware of the political and social concerns that were at the heart of the drama's focus, the high school students also saw the work as a powerful example for developing and exploring characterization and uncovering subtext. Good drama, based on strong literature, can work at most levels.

How the Story Drama Structures Work

Each structure is laid out in the same way. We begin by offering a rationale for the choice of the story. Within the rationale, we describe themes, applications, and suitability.

■   **Key Understandings and Questions** lie at the heart of the story and provide the direction of the drama and the reference points for reflection. Drama works best when the affective and the effective are integrated as universal understandings or questions; these may differ, depending on a person's experience, interests, and culture.

The organization of each activity is consistent throughout. We give each activity a number and a title and suggest approximate times.

■   **Grouping** refers to the class configuration (e.g., pairs, whole group).

■   **Strategy** names the activity; the description of the strategy is embedded in the teacher talk/instruction. We have included a concise explanation of each strategy in the Glossary for further reference.

■ **Administration** includes the space requirements as well as specific materials required for the activity.

■ **Focus** provides the *why* or objective of the activity and answers that question, "Why are we doing this?" or, "Why are you doing this with your students?"

■ **Options** are activities that we offer either as an adaptation or alternative activity for, say, younger students or as a means of extending literacy skills using the drama as a meaningful context.

■ **Extensions** are based on specific activities that teachers have used to extend the drama experience or to integrate it into other curriculum areas.

■ **Resources** provide you with references for either the teacher or the students.

■ A summary list of **Materials** according to strategy acts as a quick and useful reminder.

■ **Reflection** is an important part of effective drama. It occurs *throughout* the structures, sometimes as a way to think about where we have been in order to know where we are and/or where we need to go. Reflection also serves as a way of processing what has happened and, especially in the final activities, to help us move beyond the particulars of the story to the more universal implications.

■ **Questions** are another important component of drama and are used extensively throughout. The questions that stimulate the most effective thought are open, allowing students to contribute their own ideas and appreciate the perspectives and ideas of others.

The structures serve teachers as complete frameworks of organization for understanding how strategies and techniques can be used to deepen the drama. They offer examples of how one activity is linked to another. Linking is a critical means of achieving coherence in the flow of meaning, not only for the students, but also for the teacher. Linking activities to create a dramatic flow that moves the story forward while at the same time deepening meaning is fundamental to effective drama and is rarely addressed in the literature of practice. Linking is one of the most important elements in planning drama.

The structures also demonstrate how to introduce symbolic elements and how they accumulate significance in the drama world. For example, in a structure based on *The Pumpkin Blanket* (Zagwÿn 1995), the students may not be aware on a cognitive level of the significance of the blanket as a symbol for recognizing the needs of others. Nevertheless, the design of the structure makes it possible for children to recognize that the giving up of the blanket to keep the pumpkins warm is, as a grade-two student said, "like giving up a piece of yourself."

The detailed instructions for the individual activities can provide templates for use in other situations. As teachers and students become more comfortable using the structures, they will soon see how to apply drama strategies to other contexts. One teacher reported that, after experiencing hot seating (questioning someone in role) in a story drama structure based on Booth's *The Dust Bowl* (1996), her students suggested this strategy as a "great" activity for their novel study. The students, through their drama experience, were becoming aware of drama strategies and of drama's potential to open up learning in other areas. This experienced teacher felt confident enough to act on their suggestion and to use a "high risk" (for her) drama strategy.

The structures demonstrate the effectiveness of questioning as a way of creating and/or deepening engagement. Reflection time and discussion questions focus on the stories' "hot" or dramatic moments. Thinking about what made those moments memorable enables participants to talk together about the different ways of creating dramatic tension. The reflection strategies and questions engender wider thinking and opportunities for personal and generalized application. It is the reflection at the end of each structure that helps students make connections to the key understandings that lie at the heart of the work.

Classroom Implementation

The drama structures in this book all take between an hour and fifteen minutes and three hours. They need time to unfold. Many teachers have their class do only two or three activities at a time and often take as long as a week to complete the drama part of a larger curriculum unit. Use the suggested times given for the activities as a guideline: the time you actually take will depend upon the skills of the students, their interest, and the importance of the activity to your curriculum objectives and to learner needs. Because we see these structures as one way of integrating curriculum, they can be taught as an introduction to content, as a means of expanding the content, or as a means of applying new knowledge.

Of course, you can read the story and use only one or two activities to extend the experience for your students. This is a good way to begin doing drama especially if it is new to you. If you want to use the whole structure, remember that what might be regarded as "boring" or "non-drama" bits are important. Initial activities that involve such strategies as drawing or playing a game and which, perhaps, may seem extraneous, are included for a reason. It takes time for us to construct a fictional world and, in drama, there are many ways to effect what is called, "building belief" (Wagner 1999). If your class time is limited, these introductory activities can be done the day before in preparation for entering the story.

When we are teaching a drama structure, we carry a copy of it with us in a format that makes it easy to follow. Sometimes, teachers will copy the structure onto note cards; some will use an outline. There is no rule that a teacher has to follow the structure word for word, as long as he or she feels confident about the main points. And, although it may seem that there is a great deal of teacher talk, much of the talking is talking *in role*. In our experience, students listen differently to each other and to the teacher when they are in role, possibly because they *need to know*; what is being said is important to their understanding of the situations in which they find themselves. When we are working as "teacher in role," we will often have the specific words from the structure written out on a note card to ensure that we are feeding in the information that will generate the tension. For example, in All Dried Up and Blown Away, when the farmer says, "Too hot to work in the day, too hot to sleep at night," it puts us all into an affective recognition of the situation. "I've borrowed money, as we always do, to buy seed" sets up the letter from the bank manager calling in the loan. As teacher in role, you give students the information they need and suggest or introduce the implications of that information. When working in role, the less you say, the more your students are pressed into speech.

The writing-in-role strategy for All Dried Up and Blown Away *enabled Jon, a grade five student, to start to put down words on paper in a way that he had never done before. The words flowed and continued to flow through that evening at home. He showed his mother what he had written and asked, "Have I written enough?" She asked, "Have you said all you need to say?" That question started the writing again. Since then, he continues to write and write both in school and at home. Almost a year later, Jon remembers it was the drama "that made me want to write more."* (Teacher, parent, and student

Some General Guidelines

■ If you and your students are starting drama for the first time, it's a good idea to prepare them for the experience. You might want to tell them that you are all going to be doing drama together and that you (the teacher) will be playing with them. Even though the students will be inside the drama fiction, regular classroom behavior is expected (for example: working well as a group; listening as well as speaking; accepting the "as if" world of the drama—in other words, suspending disbelief). Neelands (1984) refers to this rule-setting as the "drama contract" (27).

■ You will see that all of the structures are written in action language. The instructions themselves are subsumed in the teacher talk. Students' intended action or response is given in brackets. Any teaching points that might need clarification appear in italics.

■ Integral to effective drama practice are the opportunities for students to "side-chat." When they talk to the person next to them, they are practicing and trying out their ideas in a private forum before speaking more publicly. Sometimes, side-chat is used as a way of reflecting on what's happening without having to share with the larger group.

■ Try not to be concerned if students don't jump right in. Many have learned "the rules of school": be quiet; don't talk; stay in your desk. We know that classrooms are changing but you only have to watch young children "play school" to know that these rules are almost neurologically programmed.

■ If you are not sure of what is going on, stop and ask. The students usually are able to tell you what is happening, what needs to happen, and how to make it happen. Sometimes teachers new to drama think that if it is interrupted, the drama will be ruined. Not so. When children play, they go in and out of role all the time.

Finally, if you take the work seriously, your students will begin to understand that the "fun" is in the doing and in making it happen.

When Carole was new to role drama, she and her grade-ten students arrived at the end of the drama (according to the book) but the students were not ready to stop. She telephoned her colleague Juliana. "What do I do now?" Juliana, not having a clue herself, said, "Ask them." Carole did, and the drama went on until everyone was satisfied that they had explored all they needed.

Assessing Effectiveness

When we are looking for a way to assess a book, a strategy, a structure, or a way of working, the thinking of Raths, Pancella, and Van Ness (1971) often guides our decisions. They suggest that "other things being equal, one activity is more worthwhile than another" if it

■ permits students to make informed choices in carrying out the activity and to reflect on the consequences of their choices

■ assigns students active roles in the learning situation rather than passive ones

■ asks students to engage in inquiry into ideas, application of intellectual processes, or current problems, or to examine them in a new setting

■ recognizes that completion of the activity may be accomplished successfully by students at several different levels of ability

■ involves students and teachers in risk-taking
(Adapted by Daphne Morris)

Every story has a dramatic shape of some sort designed to attract listeners into a world of our making. (Booth 1999, 150)

These ideas about what is significant for effective learning apply to the aims and objectives of drama. They are also excellent prompts for reflecting on classroom drama work, either as it is happening or when it is completed.

A student we know wrote in her drama journal that "it is one thing to read a story, but it is far different to be fully engaged in one. It is as if I fell right into the storybook" (Alexandra 2002). Story drama structures offer a powerful way of putting language into action. We hope that they will help you and your students fall right into the pages of the stories, and that they give you the confidence and encouragement to create your own.

CHAPTER TWO

On-the-Way-to-Big

Based on *The Pumpkin Blanket*
written and illustrated by Deborah Turney Zagwÿn

Why Did We Choose This Story?

■ *The Pumpkin Blanket* addresses themes of caring, of responsibility, and of growing up. It is written in language that is rich, poetic, and evocative.

■ The illustrations are by the author who is an accomplished artist. There is a wide palate of color; the design is simple and accessible and captures both the innocence and the complexity of being a child.

■ The story is about a time of the year that is always celebrated in school, but it brings a new perspective to the season. It is suitable particularly for those teachers who want to acknowledge Halloween in ways that are different.

■ *The Pumpkin Blanket* can be seen as a resource for the integration of curricula, opening possibilities for any number of language and visual arts activities. The drama allows each child to enter the story in role and thereby engages the child in thinking and feeling as an "other"—the practice of empathy. The text offers children multiple means of internalizing and interpreting the story.

■ This is a story about a child who holds something to be very dear. It is about letting that something go so that it might serve another. It is about having the courage to make a decision and then to carry it through. Young children will identify with Clee's dilemma as they themselves share many of the same attachments.

Key Understandings and Questions

■ We all have things that "speak to [us] of friends, and love and serenity and dreams." (Zagwÿn 1995)

- There are moments in life that serve to transform us as we move from "just-past-small, on- [our]-way-to-Big." (Zagwÿn 1995)
- What is the true meaning of gift giving?

1. Putting on our drama hats 10–15 minutes

Grouping:	**Whole group**
Strategy:	**Transformation (scarf)**
Administration:	**A large square piece of supple fabric, all one color, that should have some substance to it**
Focus:	**To prepare for the drama world**

Teacher: Before we begin our drama, we are going to have to warm up our imaginations.

So, rub your hands together; rub very, very, very quickly, then place them on your head to get our imaginations going. [Students like to do this twice]

I have a scarf here and, because I am using my imagination, I can make it anything I want it to be. And when I make it, you're going to be able to tell what it is. Watch very carefully.

Teacher picks up the scarf, cradles it, rocks it, and passes it very gently to the child next to him or her.

Teacher: What did you see in your imagination? [They reply: "A baby"]

Yes, we all saw that it was a baby.

So, everyone take a moment to think about how you could transform this scarf into something else. Imagine hard. Yes, yes, I can see your imaginations really working!

I'm going to start again. This time, I have to stand up to show you my new idea.

It is important that the teacher models a variety of ways to transform the scarf, from both a sitting and standing position, otherwise the children may be limited in their response.

Teacher again demonstrates, using the scarf as a balance beam to walk across.

Teacher: Now, I will pass the scarf on to the person next to me and it will be their turn.

After everyone has had a turn, teacher places the scarf in the middle of the circle.

Teacher: Does anyone have another idea to transform the scarf? [Some children will take the opportunity to have another turn]

Grouping:	**Whole group**
Strategy:	**Mime**
Administration:	**None**
Focus:	**To provide the context and begin to deepen engagement**

Teacher:

Now that we have our imaginations warmed up, and you did so well imagining the scarf as something else, we're ready to use our imaginations in another way.

Think about something you have now that is really precious to you. Something that is small enough to hold in your hands. You need to find a special thing that you could, if you had to, give away.

Use your imagination to think about the questions I am going to ask you.

Pick up your precious object in your hands. What does it feel like? Is it soft or hard, or somewhere in between? Is it smooth, is it rough? Is it round or square? What is its shape; what is its color?

Where did it come from and why is it so precious to you?

I'd like you to turn to the person next to you. Make sure that you have enough room to work without disturbing others.

Just put your precious object down beside you for a moment and listen.

First decide which of you is going to be A and which of you is going to be B. In a moment, you are going to give your precious object to your partner. Try to hand it to your partner in such a way that your partner will know something about it—how heavy it is; perhaps its shape or its size. Remember, this is not a guessing game.

Partners need to be very careful when they receive this precious object and handle it with care.

As, as you hand your precious object to your partner, describe it and tell them something about it. You will have a minute to do this.

To As: Are you ready to pick up your precious object and hand it carefully to B? Good, off you go! [They do the first exchange]

Now, Bs, it is your turn. As, remember to be careful and to listen to what your partner is telling you. [They do the second exchange]

Let's hear about some of those precious gifts that you just received.

The teacher comments on the variety of things that we hold dear.

Teacher:

I wonder why you might want to give away something that is precious to you? [They offer suggestions]

Teacher validates each contribution with a comment.

Teacher:

I think we are ready now to begin our story.

3. Meeting Clee

Grouping:	**Whole group**
Strategy:	**Predicting**
Administration:	**Overhead projector; overhead of picture of Clee sitting on her bed (p. 18 of the story)**
Focus:	**To explore the picture**

Teacher: I'd like you to look very carefully at one of the pictures from our story.

Bedrooms are very important places.

Note: In the following question/response activity, if a student says, "It's fall," you might want to ask, "How do we know that?" This helps children to "read" nonverbal or illustrative information in a more detailed way.

Teacher: What is it that you notice about the bedroom?

How is it like your own room?

What do you notice about the girl in the picture?

What might she be thinking about?

What is the feeling or mood in the picture?

Now that we have so many ideas about the picture, I wonder if you have any suggestions as to what this story might be about? Talk to your partner. [They do]

Let's hear some of those ideas. [They offer; teacher comments]

4. Listen to the wind

Grouping:	**Whole group**
Strategy:	**Soundscape**
Administration:	**Small tambourine with a skin**
Focus:	**To create the atmosphere for listening and to give a sense of reality to the wind, an important element in the story**

Teacher: Remember some of you noticed through the window, the falling leaves being blown by the wind? The wind is very important all through our story. I wonder if we could create the sound of the wind as it softly and gently blows the leaves outside the window.

Sometimes it is easier if we close our eyes and just listen to the sound of the wind as we create it.

While you are making the sound of the wind, I'll make the sound of the leaves as they scratch against the windowpane.

Teacher taps fingernails against the skin of the tambourine as children make the sound of the wind.

Teacher: Perfect! Your soundscape of the wind will be the background for our story. And now we are ready to listen to Clee's story.

5. Introducing the story   *5 minutes*

Grouping:	**Whole group**
Strategy:	**Story reading aloud (teacher)**
Administration:	**The storybook**
Focus:	**To listen**

Teacher introduces the book by showing the cover, reading the title, and giving the author's name.

Teacher:	Our author grew up and lives in British Columbia and she is not only the author but she is the illustrator as well. Are we ready to listen?
Teacher reads from beginning of the story to:	*Finally, Clee had only one square left. It was her favorite, the one with the widest satin edge, soft and dreamy between her fingers, and smooth under her cheek.*

6. Moving into role   *5 minutes*

Grouping:	**Individuals in own space**
Strategy:	**Building role**
Administration:	**None**
Focus:	**To build belief and commitment**

Teacher:	For the next part of the story, I'd like you to find your own space in the room and sit down. [They do] As I turn the page, I think you will recognize the picture that we looked at earlier.

Teacher holds up the picture as she continues reading.

Teacher reads:	*Clee had only one square left. It was her favorite. . . . That day, Clee did not go down to the garden with her father. She sat on her bed and looked down at the pumpkin patch.*
Teacher:	Let's all imagine that we are Clee, looking out of the window and seeing with her eyes.
Teacher reads:	*Eleven pumpkins wore eleven little blankets. The twelfth pumpkin was bare. It was the biggest pumpkin of all and the last one to be uncovered by the vines. . . .* *Clee sat all day by her window [and] clutched her tiny pumpkin blanket tightly in her hand. She watched the wind blowing the dead leaves in circles around the pumpkins. The vines stiffened with cold. Darkness was falling on the garden.*
Teacher:	Imagine what Clee is thinking as she holds the very last piece of her pumpkin blanket in her hands.
Pause.	
Teacher:	Something else needs the blanket's protection and Clee is old enough and wise enough to know what she has to do.

Grouping:	**Individuals in own space**
Strategies:	**Movement; reenacting**
Administration:	**Light dimmed; tambourine**
Focus:	**To listen and respond physically**

<u>Teacher:</u> In role as Clee, pay attention to the words that I am going to read now. They will guide you and tell you what to do.

In a moment, we will all stand up and become Clee as she carries out her decision. We will all be moving as Clee.

Be sure, as you move, that you focus only on what *you* are doing. This will take lots of concentration and you will have to really use your imaginations to help you to make it real. Clee, are you ready? Let's begin.

Teacher reads, using the tambourine skin for tapping and brushes a hand in a circular fashion on the skin to create the sound of the leaves, the branches, and the wind. Note: Teacher adjusts the pace of the reading to accommodate the children's movements. It's important to pause between descriptions of each action, giving students time to respond as Clee.

<u>Teacher:</u> Clee stood up and slipped on her sweater.

She tiptoed down the hall to the door and opened it.

It was dark and chilly outside. She wrapped her arms around herself to keep herself from shivering. The wind was blowing and the bare branches of the trees scraped against the house.

Leaves brushed against Clee as she walked slowly toward the garden.

She stopped by the big pumpkin. The bare pumpkin glowed in the moonlight. Clee bent down and touched its icy shell.

Stop sound of the tambourine.

<u>Teacher:</u> The wind suddenly stopped. All was silent.

Speak a little more slowly, as the children do as the text says.

<u>Teacher:</u> Clee tucked her last scrap of pumpkin blanket round the biggest pumpkin of all. She looked at what she had done.

Then she heard the wind starting up again.

Restart the sound on the tambourine.

<u>Teacher:</u> She turned and ran back to the house before she could change her mind.

Rattle the tambourine as they run back to their places.

<u>Teacher:</u> Phew! She had done it!

Back in her room, she sat on her bed looking out at all the pumpkins. Each one had its own pumpkin blanket. She thought about what she had just done and how she felt.

8. Clee thinks about what she has just done   5–7 minutes

Grouping:	**Individuals**
Strategy:	**Tapping in**
Administration:	**None**
Focus:	**To reflect in role**

Teacher: Clee, close your eyes and think about what you have just done. [They do]

In a moment, when I come around and touch your shoulder, we will hear your thoughts. When you have finished speaking, drop your head and cover your eyes, then I'll know who has spoken.

Teacher moves around the room, gently touching individual children on the shoulder and asking, Clee, what are you thinking?

Note: It is helpful to the children if you leave your hand on their shoulders as they speak.

After all children have spoken, teacher acknowledges their contributions.

Teacher: Thank you. That was a very difficult decision that Clee made. It must have also been quite scary to go out on that dark night. She had a lot of courage. Let's get ready to hear the rest of the story now.

9. The end of the story   2 minutes

Grouping:	**Whole group**
Strategy:	**Reading aloud (teacher)**
Administration:	**The storybook**
Focus:	**To listen to how the author concludes the story**

Teacher reads from: *Clee missed her pumpkin blanket* to the end of the story.

Students should be close enough to see the pictures in the book as teacher holds it up.

Teacher: When we first met Clee sitting on her bed, we didn't know too much about her. Since we've all become Clee, we know a lot more about the kind of person she is. I wonder what words we could use to describe her?

10. Who is Clee?   5 minutes

Grouping:	**Whole group**
Strategy:	**Role on the wall**
Administration:	**Cut out life-size silhouette of Clee made of craft paper; felt pens, if the children have writing skills**
	OR
	The outline of Clee on the blackboard; chalk
Focus:	**To synthesize students' understanding; to use adjectives in context**

Teacher records (or students write) inside outline the descriptive words that reveal their understanding of the character.

Grouping:	**Whole group**
Strategy:	**Reflection**
Administration:	**None**
Focus:	**Personal application**

Use one or more questions below, as needed. It is important to leave enough time for reflection on the story that the children have just experienced. This is where the learning moves beyond immediate concerns into the wider application of the learning and the possibilities for later transfer.

Teacher: When I look at all the words you have used to describe Clee, I can see that so many of them apply to all of you. As I read them aloud, think of the ones that fit you.

Teacher reads list of descriptive words.

Teacher: Clee made a very important decision. What does her decision to give up the last piece of her pumpkin blanket tell us about giving?

                      We all give presents, at Christmas, at birthdays—but somehow this seems to be different. I wonder what makes this gift different?

If appropriate:

                      We know that Halloween is in a couple of days. How is this story different from other Halloween stories that we know?

Extensions

1. *Making a Pumpkin Blanket*

Children create a pumpkin blanket, using 12-inch squares of cotton fabric (or paper) and fabric paints, crayons, or felt markers.

Children may then title their squares and/or write the story of their square.

Teacher may then assemble all the squares as a quilt and hang the pumpkin blanket on the classroom wall or outside the classroom in the hallway.

2. *Creating Found Poems*

This story's language makes it a perfect source for found poetry.

Teacher rereads the story and children record the words that appeal to them.

Children pair up and combine the words that they enjoyed into a poem they make together.

OR

If the children are not yet writers, the teacher records their word suggestions. As a class, these words can then be manipulated into a free-verse poem.

Resources

Crayola Art Techniques. 1991. Binney & Smith, PO Box 431, Easton, PA.

Kids Making Quilts for Kids. 1992. ABC Quilts. Quilt Digest Press.

Swartz, L. 1993. *Classroom Events Through Poetry*. Markham, ON: Pembroke.

Zagwÿn, D. T. 1995. *The Pumpkin Blanket*. Markham, ON: Fitzhenry & Whiteside.

Materials

We assume that you will have a chalkboard and chalk available.

Activity 1:   Soft supple fabric scarf

Activity 3:   Overhead projector; overhead of the picture of Clee sitting on her bed

Activity 4:   Small tambourine with a skin

Activity 10:   Life-size outline cutout of Clee, felt pens

Extension 1:   12-inch fabric squares (one for each child); fabric crayons or 12-inch paper squares (one for each child) and crayons or felt marker

CHAPTER THREE

Suppose a Wolf Came Out of the Forest?

Based on *Peter and the Wolf*
retold and illustrated by Michèle Lemieux

Why Did We Choose This story?

■ *Peter and the Wolf* is a story about a child who disobeys an adult and the consequences of that behavior. It is about abandonment and rejoining, about disobedience and courage, and about the love between parents, grandparents, and children.

■ In this retelling of a classic tale that has appeal for adults and students alike, the writing style follows the illustrations in that it is easily understood and appreciated without being simplistic.

■ The illustrations are from an award-winning Canadian illustrator. There is a rich use of color; the design is simple but the use of perspective gives a complexity well within students' capacity to absorb.

■ The material in the story can help to deepen understanding in terms of specific curriculum. Suppose a Wolf Came Out of the Forest? can be seen as a resource for the integration of curricula. The drama incorporates language, literacy, and visual arts activities and engages students in authentic encounters with the ideas and dilemmas of environmental education and social studies. In addition, there are opportunities for students to research environmental issues, endangered species, and the responsibilities of caring for animals.

Key Understandings and Questions

■ Each one of us has the ability to do the right thing.
■ Disobedience has consequences.
■ All animals, like human beings, share basic needs: family; shelter; protection; water and food.
■ What is the place of zoos in our society?

1. Putting on our drama hats   *10–15 minutes*

Grouping:	**Whole group**
Strategy:	**Transformation (jacket)**
Administration:	**A soft leather jacket, brown, gray, or black**
Focus:	**To enter the drama world**

Note: The following activity is the same one that we used in the previous drama. In drama, we always do things more than once and this activity is one that everybody loves. The jacket offers different possibilities and also different challenges. As well, the activity provides practice for the strategy used in Activity 3— Creating the Wolf—where the jacket becomes the central symbol for the drama.

Teacher: Before we begin our drama, we are going to have to warm up our imaginations.

So, rub your hands together; rub very, very, very quickly, then place them on your head to get our imaginations going. [Students like to do this twice]

We're going to begin by doing a short activity so that we're really warmed up.

I have a jacket here and because I am using my imagination, I can make it anything I want it to be. And when I create it, you're going to be able to tell what it is. Watch very carefully.

Teacher picks up the jacket and wraps the arms around her waist.

Teacher: What did you see in your imagination? [They reply: "An apron"]

Yes, we could all see that it was an apron.

So, everyone take a moment to think about how you could transform this jacket into something else. Imagine hard. Yes, yes, I can see your imaginations really working!

I'm going to start again. This time, I have to stand up to show you my new idea. Then I will pass the jacket on to the person next to me and then it will be their turn.

Teacher again demonstrates, this time using the jacket as a dance partner. It is important that the teacher models a variety of ways to transform the jacket, otherwise the students may be limited in their response. After everyone has had a turn, teacher places the jacket in the middle of the circle.

Teacher: Does anyone have another idea to transform the jacket? [Some take the opportunity to have another turn]

2. Reading the story 7–10 *minutes*

Grouping:	**Whole group**
Strategy:	**Reading aloud (teacher)**
Administration:	**The storybook**
Focus:	**To provide the context and begin to deepen engagement**

Teacher:	Now that we have our imaginations warmed up, we're ready for our story. Come and sit closer, where you can see the pictures.
	Listen carefully and use your imaginations as we enter the story.
Teacher reads from beginning to:	*What kind of bird are you if you can't fly? What kind of bird are you, if you can't swim?*
Teacher:	I wonder what kind of bird that could possibly be? [They provide suggestions]
Teacher continues the story to:	*Don't shoot. The bird and I have already caught the wolf.*

Teacher closes the book.

Teacher narrates:	And the hunters didn't kill the wolf but shot her with a sleeping dart, so that she would not be hurt while they decided what to do with her.

3. Creating the wolf 7 *minutes*

Grouping:	**Whole group**
Strategy:	**Designing**
Administration:	**Soft leather jacket**
Focus:	**To build commitment and belief in the wolf**

Teacher places the jacket on the floor in the center of the room.

Teacher:	I wonder how we could arrange this jacket so that we can all agree that it is the sleeping wolf.
	Does anyone have an idea of how we could do that? [They come forward and arrange the jacket]
	Everyone needs to be watching because when we finish, we will all have to agree that this is the sleeping wolf. [They continue to arrange the jacket until they are satisfied]
	Are we all agreed that this is the sleeping wolf? [They agree]
	Who would be willing to help me move the wolf over to the side so that we don't awaken it during our drama?

Moving the wolf carefully is one step in helping to build belief and elevate the "jacket" into a symbol.

22   *Chapter Three*

4. Remembering how it used to be

Grouping:	**Whole group**
Strategy:	**Improvisation**
Administration:	**None**
Focus:	**To move into role to create the people of the village**

Teacher: I'd like you to imagine that you are the people who live in the village where this wolf was just caught.

Can you remember a time when there were no wolves roaming the forest and everything was safe? A time when nothing could possibly hurt us?

I remember when I could go out for walks at any time. There were no wolves then. Those times were good, safe times. Things have certainly changed.

Well. What are we going to do about this wolf? It's just not safe here anymore. Now that we've caught it, we can't just let it go. It's dangerous for everyone, especially our children.

Note: When students are offering suggestions [e.g.,"Put it back in the forest," "Put it in the fair," "Put it in the zoo," "Kill it," "Make a coat from the skin"], it's important to accept all their ideas without judgment, although the students themselves may have something to say about each other's ideas!

5. Unforeseen complications

Grouping:	**Whole group**
Strategy:	**Teacher in role as a concerned citizen**
Administration:	**None**
Focus:	**To introduce complexity**

Teacher: And I understand there is another problem. The hunters, who were out in the woods, found a pack of baby cubs all by themselves. They were crying and howling for their mother.

The hunters left the little cubs in their den but who knows how long they will survive without their mother? They looked as if they had just been born. I didn't realize she had just had babies. They need their mother!

If there is another adult in the classroom, you can use him or her to introduce the complication; i.e.: "I've just been walking in the woods and came upon a pack of newly born wolf cubs" (as above).

Teacher: What are we going to do now? Now we have the cubs to worry about. [They offer suggestions]

You will find that they have many ideas. If the idea of the zoo is introduced, teacher picks it up.

Teacher: I don't remember a time in our zoo when they had a wolf, let alone baby cubs. Do you think the zookeeper will let us bring them along too? What should we do? [They offer suggestions]

OR

If students don't offer the zoo as a possibility, you can say contemplatively,

<u>Teacher:</u>	I wonder if the zoo would be willing to take the wolf and her cubs. They'd be safe there, I know, and we would be safe as well. Do you think the zookeeper will let us bring them along too? What should we do? [They offer suggestions]

Teacher listens carefully and validates the suggestions, asking for elaboration if needed. Before the discussion wanes,

<u>Teacher:</u>	I wonder if we could write a letter and persuade the zookeeper to let us present the wolf and her cubs to the zoo.
	What will we say in our letter?

6. Finding solutions   7–10 *minutes*

Grouping: **Pairs**
Strategy: **Writing in role**
Administration: **Paper and pencil for each pair**
Focus: **To explore how we can persuade another**

<u>Teacher:</u>	While I bring you paper, talk to your neighbor about how you will convince the zookeeper to take the wolf and her cubs.

Students talk together while teacher distributes materials.

<u>Teacher:</u>	Let's hear some of your ideas before we begin. [They share]

You don't need to hear from everyone. The sharing serves as a prompt for those who are having difficulty.

<u>Teacher:</u>	Begin writing your letter when you are ready.

Time for this activity is dependent upon the skills of the students and the importance of the activity to your learning objectives or learner needs.

OR

Teacher may use the activity for the whole class to compose a letter together. In that case,

Grouping: **Whole group**
Strategy: **Writing in role**
Administration: **Easel, chart paper, and black felt pen for the teacher**
Focus: **To explore how we can persuade another**

<u>Teacher:</u>	How shall we begin our letter to the zookeeper?

Proceed as above, using suggestions as prompts to complete letter.

<u>Teacher:</u>	Thank you for these (this) letter(s). I am sure that anyone reading these words would have a hard time refusing our request.
<u>Teacher narrates:</u>	And the letter(s) reached the zookeeper. Soon the people of the village received an invitation to visit the zoo and speak to the zookeeper.

| Teacher: | Will you agree that when I put on these glasses (this hat) and sit in this chair, I will be the zookeeper? [They agree] |

Teacher places chair in front of the students and sits.

7. A visit with the zookeeper   5 minutes

Grouping:	**Whole group**
Strategy:	**Teacher in role as zookeeper**
Administration:	**Students' letters; glasses or a hat for the zookeeper; chair**
Focus:	**To honor the villagers' concerns but not to make it easy for them to turn the problem over to someone else; to encourage thinking about environmental habitats**

| Teacher: | I'd like to welcome you villagers to the zoo. I'm sorry to have kept you waiting but I hope that you have had a chance to visit your favorite animals. I wonder what you saw that you enjoyed most? [Some students may offer]

Now, to your letter(s). I understand that you have been faced with a problem and I am very interested in what you have to say. For instance, you wrote . . . |

If more than one letter, teacher does not need to read every one but just enough to validate their skills at persuasion, perhaps asking for clarification to challenge suggestions. If one letter, teacher reads it aloud, asking for clarification and elaboration as needed.

| Teacher: | You need to understand things from the zoo's point of view. We've never had wolves here before. We have lots of elephants, lions, kangaroos—but never any wolves.

We don't know how to look after them. Where would we put them? What would we feed them? I need more information to give to the zoo committee.

I can't make these decisions on my own without some suggestions. You people seem to have a lot of good ideas. I wonder if you could help me by creating some plans that I could show to the zoo committee?

What sort of habitat will the wolves need? Remember, we will need to think of the cubs, as well as their mother.

If you could just sketch out some ideas, it would be very helpful. After all, we can't just let wolves roam around. They can be very dangerous. We need to make sure that we are all safe and at the same time, find a solution for the wolves too.

Thanks very much for meeting with me. I will let you get busy on your designs and go and tell my committee what they can expect.

Goodbye and thank you for your letters. It is good to see your concerns for these beautiful animals. |

Teacher gets up, takes off glasses (or hat), and moves to another part of the room.

8. Working as habitat designers — 7–10 minutes

Grouping:	**Groups of 3–4, depending on age and social skills**
Strategy:	**Designing**
Administration:	**17-by-22-inch paper; felt pens**
Focus:	**To concretize ideas**

Teacher assigns groups or students choose groups. Use only one sheet of paper per group and multiple pens. Teacher encourages designers by moving around and commenting on and questioning the designs. When groups are almost finished, teacher asks each group to choose one or two villagers to present the design to the zookeeper.

9. Presentation of the designs to the zookeeper — 7 minutes

Grouping:	**Whole group**
Strategy:	**Presentation**
Administration:	**Student designs**
Focus:	**To develop oral language**

Teacher:
We are ready to present our designs. Some of you have agreed to show your group's designs to the zookeeper. Is that right? I know the zookeeper is waiting to hear your plans for the wolf habitat.

When I sit down in this chair, I will become the zookeeper again. Are we ready?

Teacher puts on zookeeper glasses (or hat) and sits.

Teacher in role as zookeeper:
Thank you for working so quickly. We're under a lot of pressure. The wolf will soon wake up and her cubs need to be fed. Which villagers are prepared to present their designs?

I look forward to hearing and seeing your plans. [Students come forward, usually two from the group, and hold the design up for the others to see, explaining their design.]

Teacher as zookeeper may or may not comment or question but always acknowledges and validates ideas and the work. Young children may only be able to listen to two or three at a time.

Teacher:
Villagers, you have worked very hard indeed. Our zoo committee has a lot of difficult decisions to make. I'm afraid I can't give you a decision immediately but we will study your designs. Please leave them with me. In the meantime, I will look after the wolf and her cubs and make sure that you villagers are safe.

Goodbye and thank you again for being so concerned and so helpful.

Teacher gets up, takes off glasses (or hat), and moves away.

10. *Slipping back into the world of the classroom* *6 minutes*

Grouping:	**Whole group**
Strategy:	**Coming out of role**
Administration:	**None**
Focus:	**To take off our drama hats**

Teacher:

I wonder what the committee will decide.

Those villagers had so many ideas. I know that they will find a solution that will be good for the zoo, good for the wolves, and good for the villagers.

So, we have just about finished our drama and when we rub our hands together and put them on our heads, we will be back in the classroom.

Are we ready?

Teacher models; students follow.

Teacher:

Well, that was fun! And such hard work!

Talk to the person next to you about what you remember most about our drama. [They talk together]

Who would like to share with the group?

The sharing is opened up to the whole group. It is here that ideas expressed in Understandings and Key Questions can be folded in and assimilated.

Two suggestions:

Teacher:

In our story, the people of the village needed to find a way to take care of themselves and the wolves, especially those cubs who couldn't take care of themselves alone. You know, our classroom is something like that village. We don't have dangerous animals to worry about but sometimes we need to look after one another. How can we manage to do that—to help all of us feel safe and secure?

When we were designing our habitats for the wolves, we needed to remember what they would require to live in a healthy environment. Let's make a list of the wolves' needs. [They do] I wonder what needs students have that are the same or different from the wolves?

OR

When I was growing up, there were never any questions about whether or not zoos were a good thing. That was where we went to see all kinds of animals, especially those that come from faraway places, like tigers and elephants. Can you think of others? [They suggest]

Now some people question whether or not zoos are good places for these animals. Should we be putting animals that are used to roaming the land in small spaces? Some zoos have created "natural" habitats to keep the animals happy. What do you think about animals in zoos?

Other drama strategies you could explore

1. Students as wolves, prowling the forest and the village. (Movement)
2. Rumors about the wolf. What have we heard? (Gossip mill)
3. Speaking the thoughts of the wolf as it prowls the village. (Voice collage)
4. Creating pictures of what the village was like before the wolf. (Tableau)
5. Listening to appropriate music (e.g., Sergei Prokofiev's *Peter and the Wolf*). Here the students become acquainted with the various instruments of the orchestra and how music can tell a story.

Potential cross-curricular follow-up activities

1. Students convert their initial habitat designs into three-dimensional models.
2. Students devise strategies for the protection of endangered species.
3. Students devise a public-information poster aimed at the children of the village to alert them to the dangers of the wolf.
4. Group researches the kinds of food that would be required for a healthy wolf diet.
5. Group researches wolves in North America and what is being done to save them from extinction or hunters.
6. Students consider the controversy between hunters and environmentalists.
7. Students look at other stories to see how wolves are portrayed (e.g., Little Red Riding Hood; The Three Little Pigs; The Wolf Boy).

Resources

George, J. C. *Look to the North: A Wolf Pup Diary*. New York: Trophy Picture Books, HarperCollins.

Lemieux, M. 1991. *Peter and the Wolf.* Toronto, ON: Kids Can Press.

Miller, C., A. Preece, and J. O'Mara. 1999. "Just a Jacket on the Floor?" *Language Arts.* 77 (2): 137–42.

Milton, J. *Wild Wild Wolves.* New York: Random House.

Swanson, D. *Welcome to the World of Wolves.* Toronto, ON: Whitecap Books.

Materials

We assume that you will have a chalkboard and chalk available.
A copy of the story, with stickies to mark the stopping point.

Activity 1:   Soft leather jacket
Activity 3:   Soft leather jacket

Activity 6:   Paper and pencils **or** chart paper and dark felt pen
Activity 7:   Glasses or hat
Activity 8:   17-by-22-inch paper, felt pens of various colors

Follow-Up Letter

When we work with students using this story drama structure, we often send them a letter that validates the work.

We include it as a template (Figure 3.1). Use it as you wish. The school library will have an appropriate book.

Date:

Memo to: The Villagers of —————————

From: The Zoological Committee for Expansion

Re: Wolf Habitat

Dear Villagers:

Thank you for your very convincing letter and carefully detailed designs for a wolf habitat. We were particularly impressed with your consideration of the needs of the wolf and her cubs, as well as the safety of the visitors to the zoo. We agree that with the addition of wolves to our zoo, the habitat will become an important site for researchers.

Through your action as a community, we have been able to apply for a grant that will cover the total costs (including feeding) of the wolf habitat. This would not have happened had it not been for your concerns both for the animals and for the reputation of our zoo as a leader in animal research and conservation.

Thank you again. We enclose a copy of a book that we have found useful in preparing for the wolves. We hope that you and your families will enjoy reading it. We look forward to welcoming you to the zoo.

Yours sincerely,

_____   _____

Chair: Zookeeper

Expansion Committee

FIGURE 3.1   Follow-up letter template

CHAPTER FOUR

Better Than Bed Socks

Based on *The Very Best of Friends*
written by Margaret Wild and illustrated by Julie Vivas

Why Did We Choose This Story?

■ The text, *The Very Best of Friends*, won the Children's Book Council of Australia's Picture Book of the Year (1990), and the illustrator, Julie Vivas, has become known for her portrayals of adults and children.

■ The story addresses the themes of friendship, responsibility, and loss; all are part of the written as well as the "hidden" curriculum.

■ Whether a pet is a part of a family or not, children understand the pleasure/burden that comes with assuming such responsibility.

■ Although the simplicity of the story makes it very accessible, engaging in the drama activities offers students the opportunity to begin to develop the skills of interpreting nuance both in verbal and nonverbal language.

Key Understandings and Questions

■ What is a friend?
■ Loss changes people in unexpected ways.
■ How you treat your friends and your pets may be reflected in their actions toward you.

1. Building context   15–20 minutes

Grouping:	**4–5 groups (depending upon class size) divided equally**
Strategy:	**Brainstorming**
Administration:	**Large chart paper (1 for each group) with single word written in large capitals in the middle of the page; felt markers; masking tape**
Focus:	**To build collaborative meanings**

Divide class into four or five groups. Each group is given a large sheet of paper and a number of felt pens. Each sheet has one of the following words written on it in large print:

Groups	Words
A	OUTCAST
B	FRIEND
C	BELONGING
D	THE FARM
E	HOME (if needed)

Depending upon the size of your class and their experience in group work, you may wish to have smaller groups. Generally speaking, you want to keep the groups' size to no more than six. If you feel that your class works best in smaller groups (e.g., groups of four), more than one group may interpret the same word.

Teacher: On the chart paper write down any thoughts and images that come to mind as you look at the key word on your page. It doesn't matter if you have ideas that are different. Build on each other's ideas. You will need to work quickly.

There may be some talking. The talking helps to generate ideas. Remind students that they do not have much time to complete the task. Stop after about two minutes or when you see that there are five or more words/phrases on each of the sheets.

Teacher: In a moment, I am going to ask you to move on to where the group next to you has been working.

When you get there, look at what the previous group has written and then add your ideas to the key word. For example, Group A will add their ideas on "Friend" to Group Bs initial thinking. Group B will move to Group Cs "Belonging," and Group C will move to Group Ds "Home" and so on.

Ready? Off you go.

After each group has completed the task—be sure to remind them to work quickly—the groups move on again to add their ideas to those already written on the next sheet. The rotation is completed when each group has added their "take" to the other sheets of paper and returned to their original word.

Teacher: Look at the new ideas that have been added by other people to your original comments. Talk about these and how your ideas have been expanded. [They do]

2. *Making abstract concepts concrete*

Grouping: **Same as for Activity 1**
Strategy: **Tableau**
Administration: **A working space for each group; sentence strips and felt pens**
Focus: **To use their bodies to convey meanings that are basic to the story**

<u>Teacher:</u> Take the essence of what is on your page and what you have talked about and using everyone in your group, create a still picture—a tableau—with your bodies that best represents your thinking about your key word.

This is going to be difficult because you have so many wonderful ideas. You are going to have to make some decisions about how you can represent those ideas in a still picture.

We are going to be "reading" these tableaux just as we read the words on your pages. Therefore, you need to be sure that you can hold the picture still for us while we read it.

You will need to work quickly. You have about three minutes.

Students may need more time, but it is better to limit their time to begin with and give another minute when necessary.

When the students have their tableaux prepared, arrange groups in a circle. Groups present in sequence around circle, so all students can see tableaux.

<u>Teacher:</u> Just before we begin to share, let's hang up your key-word collage. It will be a reference for our work now and later. [They do]

Before we share our tableaux, I am going to give each group a caption strip. On that strip of paper, write the title of your tableau as if it were the title of a story. How will your title help us to understand the thinking and feeling that you are showing us?

Write the caption down in large-enough print so that we can read it as we see your tableau.

As a group is getting ready to present, I will tell everyone else to close their eyes while they prepare. When I say "Open," you may open your eyes and begin to read the picture. I will remind you of the word that is being interpreted and then read the caption.

As each tableau is presented (about one minute for each),

<u>Teacher:</u> What do we see? [Students offer their ideas]

Where do you see this?

Some examples:

> <u>Student:</u> *I see people who are happy.*
> <u>Teacher:</u> *Where in the tableau do you see that?*
> <u>Student:</u> *I see it in their faces.*
> <u>Teacher:</u> *Good observation. What else do we see?* [They add]
> <u>Teacher:</u> *What does that tell us about the group's interpretation of the word "Belonging"?*

We are asking the students to say what they see and where they see it (reading the picture); to identify for all of us the specific clues that read "happy"; then, and only then, to consider the possible interpretations.

Teacher:	Thank you very much. Those were powerful tableaux and have helped us to understand what we all are thinking about when we hear the words that we have been working with.
	How we understand those words is going to be very important to us as we enter our story.

3. Entering the story   1 minute

Grouping:	**Whole group**
Strategy:	**Reading aloud (teacher)**
Administration:	**The storybook**
Focus:	**To meet the characters in the story**

Teacher reads from the beginning to:	*Cats aren't nearly as useful as dogs,* adding: *I don't like cats!*

4. How William came to live with James and Jessie   10 minutes

Grouping:	**Pairs**
Strategy:	**Improvisation**
Administration:	**None; you may wish to use a small drum or tambourine for signaling**
Focus:	**To work as authors**

Teacher:	Find a partner and together find your own space where you can work together and not disturb anyone else. Decide who will be James and who will be Jessie.
	I'd like you to imagine that this is the first time that James will introduce William, the cat, to Jessie.
	I wonder how James and William might have met? Any ideas?

Teacher encourages two or three ideas that may form the basis of the improvisation. For example: William just wandered onto the farm; a friend's cat had kittens and James took one.

Teacher:	(*To student in role as James.*) James: Take a moment to think about what you are going to say to Jessie, knowing that she may not want a cat.
	(*To student in role as Jessie.*) Jessie: You are going to be meeting William for the first time. What do you know about cats?

Give students a moment to think.

Teacher:	Now, before James and Jessie talk together, let's just test out how our stories might work.
	Turn to the pair beside you and test out your stories on each other.
	Jameses, talk together about how you and William found each other. Where was it; how did you bring William home? What's the story you are going to tell Jessie?

Jessies, you need to talk together about what story James might tell you and what questions you might ask him about William. [Students talk together for a few minutes to build their stories]

Rejoin your partner and decide who is going to speak first.

Jessie, you will have the last line. Do you remember what it is?

Some may remember; if not, repeat, **I don't like cats!**

Teacher:

"I don't like cats!" will be the last line of your improvisation and then you will sit down. We will know your scene is finished. Just sit quietly until everyone has finished and is sitting down.

Now remember, there will be lots of people speaking at once. You will really need to focus on one another and block out everyone else.

Are we ready to begin? Hands up, who has the opening line? Good. Ready? Begin.

Note: You need only give them a minute or two for the improvisation. You want to just let them have a taste of dialogue in role. It is preparation for the next strategy.

Teacher:

Talk to your partner about how true to life your conversation was.

Is there anyone who would like to share their story of how William came to live with Jessie and James? [They may share, or they may be happy to move on]

5. William finds a home   10 *minutes*

Grouping:	**Whole group**
Strategy:	**Teacher and students in role; hot seating**
Administration:	**A chair and an apron or old work shirt for Jessie**
Focus:	**To persuade Jessie**

Teacher:

In the next part of our drama, we will be imagining that we are all James. We know that Jessie is not happy about William. We also know that James really wants to keep William. How can we convince Jessie to let William stay?

Some of you may already have had an experience like this in your life. Do you remember how you persuaded your mom or dad to let you keep something? Keep that in mind but remember, James is a farmer and there are lots of animals to be looked after. William will be one more.

Think in your own mind as if you were James. What could you say to convince Jessie to let William stay? You'll need all your convincing skills when we meet Jessie.

Take time here to set this up. Students need that time to draw on their powers of persuasion. You may want to hear some of their arguments in favor of William to stimulate the thinking before moving into hot-seating Jessie.

When the students are ready, teacher brings a chair forward.

Teacher:	This will be the chair that Jessie will sit in. Let's gather round.
	Shall we sit or stand? We all need to be able to see Jessie and to hear what she has to say.

Teacher speaking as she puts on apron or shirt.

Teacher:	I am going to take on the role of Jessie and all of you will be James. I will speak first and then you will have to work really hard to find all the arguments that will change Jessie's mind.
	Who thinks they have a good reason for Jessie to agree to keep William? [Student offers] Thank you.
	Are we ready to begin?

Teacher sits on chair.

Teacher in role as Jessie:	Look, James, enough is enough. We already have animals to look after and you know I don't like cats!

Don't worry if it takes a little time for students to warm up. The key is to wait. The silence is a way of prompting them into speech. Some suggested responses for Jessie:

- Cats shed their hair all over.
- Cats scratch the furniture.
- They are smelly.
- They have to go in and out all the time.
- Who's going to feed him?
- And what are we going to feed him?
- All animals are so dependent on humans.

Don't make it easy for the students, but don't discourage them either. Students have to feel that they are being challenged, yet they need to know that their arguments are being considered. For example, in response to Jessie's comment about cats going in and out, students may suggest a cat door. Consider that as a possibility but you might want to point out that if a cat can come in and out, so could other critters. Your task here is to get them thinking "on their feet."

When you feel that the students have really given you enough, you may conclude by saying,

Teacher (in role as Jessie):	All right! Enough! We'll try it. But remember, James, William is *your* responsibility!
Teacher:	Oh, my! You were certainly convincing. Jessie didn't stand a chance against all your arguments. Well done, James!

6. Life with William, James, and Jessie   *2 minutes*

Grouping:	**Whole group**
Strategy:	**Reading aloud (teacher)**
Administration:	**The storybook**
Focus:	**To learn more**
Teacher reads from:	*Because James loved William so much,* to *Then one Sunday morning James died suddenly.*

7. Jessie's diary   5 minutes

Grouping:	**Whole group working individually**
Strategy:	**Writing in role**
Administration:	**Paper and pencils for each student**
Focus:	**To predict**

Teacher: Think about that last sentence we just heard. Quietly take a piece of paper and a pencil and find your own space and sit down.

I'd like you to imagine that you are Jessie. It is now bedtime and you have been thinking about life without James. You are sitting in your bedroom, writing in your diary about what life is like for you. Your journal is about the only thing you have to talk to now—except William. But you don't like cats!

What will you say? How has life changed since James died? What is it about your life that you will record? What will you do about William now that James is no longer here to look after him?

When you are ready, begin to write.

Let the students write for three to five minutes, depending, of course, on their writing skills. Note: Don't worry if you see them stop for a while. They may be thinking, and if you don't rush them, they will start to write again.

Teacher: Stop now and read over what you have written. Choose the sentence that you think best reflects your thinking and feeling about you and William or about life without James. Underline that sentence and memorize it.

8. Collective sharing of experience   3 minutes

Grouping:	**Whole group**
Strategy:	**Tapping in**
Administration:	**None**
Focus:	**To reflect**

Teacher: When you feel my hand on your shoulder, we will hear your words. Speak so that we can all hear you and share your thoughts. When you have finished, put your head down so that I know you have spoken.

The teacher moves randomly through the room, placing a hand (quite firmly) on a student's shoulder. Note: leave your hand there until the student has finished speaking, then move on.

After each student has contributed,

Teacher: Thank you. Life has certainly changed for Jessie.

9. How life has changed   4 minutes

Grouping:	**Whole group**
Strategy:	**Reading aloud (teacher)**
Administration:	**The storybook**
Focus:	**To learn more**

Teacher: Let's hear how our author tells the story.

Teacher reads from: *Jessie cried a lot* to *He grew mean and lean, and hated everything and everyone.*

10. Transforming into William "lean and mean"   5 minutes

Grouping:	**Pairs**
Strategy:	**Sculpting or molding**
Administration:	**Pairs work in their own spaces**
Focus:	**To translate ideas kinesthetically**

Teacher: Find a partner and a space on your own. Sit down together.

Decide who is William and who is Jessie. [They do]

Jessie, you are going to be a sculptor. Using the ideas that you heard in the story, you are going to "sculpt" your partner, William, into a lean and mean cat.

William, you are going to be a piece of clay that will be transformed by your sculptor into a lean, mean cat. Now, as clay, remember that you can't speak and you must be soft and malleable so that the sculptor can create his or her vision onto you.

Sculptors, remember, be very gentle with your partner. Do not put anyone into a position that will be hard to hold.

When we are finished, this room will be transformed into a huge exhibit of statues of lean, mean Williams.

Have the students work on their "sculpture" for about a minute.

Teacher: Thirty seconds, everyone.

Freeze, everyone.

William, your challenge now is to remain frozen. This is going to be hard and you will need to concentrate on maintaining your position. You will also need to remember how it feels for another activity later on.

What we see here is William the outcast.

Sculptors, look around the room at all the different pictures of William, the wild cat.

Sculptors, you may stop being sculptors now and return to being Jessie. Remember what she is thinking? You are alone as well.

Jessie, you are now going to position yourself in relation to William so that we can see how you feel about what is happening in your life and how you feel about William.

How will you stand or sit so that we can see how you are feeling? Take your place beside William so that we can see your relationship with William since James died.

At this point, you may want to ask half the class to "unfreeze" and look at the pictures that have been created by the other half of the class. Here you could ask, "What sorts of feelings do we see here?" Gather the answers in with interest but little comment, unless you ask, "Where do you see that?" Be sure to ask the other half of the class to "refreeze" and repeat.

Teacher:	Okay. Relax. That was hard! But we have a good idea about what Jessie and William looked like and lots of ideas about how they are feeling. Those are the marks of a good illustrator.
	Just sit down with your partner for a moment and we'll hear more of the story.

11. How life has changed   *7 minutes*

Grouping:	**Whole group**
Strategies:	**Reading aloud and tableaux transformation**
Administration:	**The storybook and tambourine or small drum**
Focus:	**To work as illustrators**
Teacher reads from:	*One morning when Jessie put out his bowl of leftovers as usual* to *He knows, deep in his heart, that Jessie is beginning to love him a lot.*
Teacher:	Relax, everyone, and listen very carefully.
	Now is the hard part. I am going to ask you to do something that you have not had a chance to practice—although we have done part of it. Are you ready?
	Take up your positions as "lean, mean William" and "Jessie alone." This is the tableau we did just before we heard this last part of the story. Focus. This is difficult work. [Students move into positions]
	Those are wonderful pictures. There is so much feeling in them.
	Just hold your poses and listen to my instructions.
	As you hear the five beats on the tambourine, *in slow motion*, you will begin to transform yourself into your new relationship—a kind of real friendship. This takes tremendous control.
	By the fifth beat, we will see Jessie and William in their new relationship. [They move to five slow beats]
	Freeze.
	Now. Just listen to the last two lines of our story.
Teacher reads:	*And late at night, when Jessie is fast asleep, William jumps onto the bed and sleeps on her feet.*
	Jessie says he is better than bed socks, any day.
Teacher:	Thinking about what you have just heard, what would be the next picture that we would see? You may each only make one move. Who

moves first and how you negotiate the new picture must be done within the five beats.

We will use the same five beats to complete the picture.

Hold your positions and stand by to transform. [They move as before to the five slow beats]

Freeze.

Let's have this half of the room relax and, staying where you are, just look around the room and see how the relationship between Jessie and William is now. [They do]

Thank you. We will reverse now so that we can see the other half of the tableaux.

Well done! Relax, everyone.

12. *Processing the experience* *as needed*

Group:	**Pairs or small groups**
Strategy:	**Discussion**
Administration:	**None, or the front cover of the story and the same picture later with William, either as is or as an overhead**
Focus:	**To reflect together, first on the themes of the drama, then on the drama experience itself**

Teacher: Just talk to your partner about that experience. [They do for a minute]

You may use any or all of the questions below but, after asking, give students a few minutes to talk, either in pairs or in small groups. It is important to let the students consider the question/s before sharing in a larger class forum.

Teacher: I wonder what it was that changed Jessie's mind about William? In the story, it simply says that William hissed and scratched her and "didn't look a bit like James's cat anymore." What do you think really changed Jessie's mind?

The story is called *The Very Best of Friends*. Let's look at this picture. What does it tell us about friendship?

Teacher shows the two pictures.

Teacher: What makes a friend a friend?

The questions above should be asked while the meaning and experience are still "hot."

The questions that follow are about how the drama worked.

Teacher: We've explored this story through drama. If you were going to choose a favorite activity that we used to explore the story, I wonder which one you would choose? [They consider together]

What was it about that activity that sticks in your mind? [They share]

Resources

Wild, M., and J. Vivas. 1990. *The Very Best of Friends*. Toronto, ON: Kids Can Press.

Materials

Activity 1:   5 sheets of chart paper, felt markers, masking tape
Activity 2:   Caption strips and felt pens
Activity 3:   The storybook
Activity 4:   A tambourine or small drum
Activity 5:   A chair, apron, or old work shirt for Jessie
Activity 6:   The storybook
Activity 7:   Paper and pencils
Activity 8:   The storybook
Activity 9:   The storybook
Activity 11: The storybook and tambourine or small drum
Activity 12: The front cover of the storybook and the later picture to which William has been added, as is or as an overhead

Alternative starting point: A tambourine or small drum

Grouping:	**Groups of 3 or 4**
Strategy:	**Tableau**
Administration:	**None; perhaps a small tambourine for signaling**
Focus:	**To represent with bodies and no language; to create a reference point to which to return at the end of the story**

Teacher:

Groups of three or four. Standing, please.

Name yourselves A, B, C, (D). [They do]

Arrange yourselves in such a way that you are using your bodies to support one another.

You have thirty seconds. [They do]

In a moment, I am going to ask one person in each group to move away from the group.

As this person is moving away, the two or three people that are left must adjust their support for each other so that they are compensating for the absence.

Try to do this compensating with as little movement as possible. We are looking at a shift of weight, rather than a significant change of positions.

Once the person has left the group and the group has compensated for the loss, freeze in your new relationship. Any questions?

I'm going to ask the Bs to move away carefully from your groups. And as you are moving away from the tableau, watch how the group is readjusting itself. Ready, everyone? Try to do this without talking.

Bs, withdraw from your groups.

Good. Groups, hold it there for the Bs to look at. [They do]

Relax. [They do]

Bs, feed back to the others your observations of what was happening. How did the group deal with the gap you left as you moved away?

As a group, talk together about what was going on in your minds as you carried out the task.

What sorts of situations can you think of in life for which this task could act as a metaphor?

What you have just been doing with your bodies tells the whole of the story we are about to explore.

Teacher returns to the story drama structure at Activity 3.

CHAPTER FIVE

Still as Stone

Based on *The Tunnel*
written and illustrated by Anthony Browne

Why Did We Choose This Story?

■ *The Tunnel* looks at family relationships in terms of siblings and their mother. For those students in single-parent families, this story validates their experience.

■ The story celebrates personality differences and breaks down the typical stereotyping that occurs in most children's perceptions of boys and girls. It is also a story about the power of love, overcoming fears, and discovering courage.

■ The story is very familiar in structure and themes. By not romanticizing the brother-and-sister relationship, the book makes it possible for students to easily identify with the protagonists. At the same time, the scenes that are not written allow students to enter and access the story by exploring the ideas based on their own experiences.

■ The illustrations by themselves provide innumerable possibilities for exploration both by what is included, what is omitted, and what is subtly indicated.

■ There are many literary references to familiar fairy and folktales and novels and stories by contemporary authors and illustrators (e.g., C. S. Lewis, Maurice Sendak).

■ *The Tunnel* can be seen as a resource for curriculum integration. There are plenty of opportunities for artwork, storying (both oral and written), and author study.

Key Understandings and Questions

■ What is it about a relationship that moves us to take actions that we might never consider taking in any other situation?

- What does a name signify? Why does the author not refer to the children by name until the very end of the book?
- A tunnel is a powerful metaphor for signifying a journey. What other stories, myths, or life experiences use a version of this metaphor?

1. Gaining interest   10–15 *minutes*

Grouping:	**Whole group**
Strategy:	**Game (Streets and Alleys)**
Administration:	**A large, open space**
Focus:	**To enter the drama world and provide a dramatic structure for later use**

Teacher: Before we begin our drama, we are going to play a game that will prepare us for our work later on in our drama. The name of the game is Streets and Alleys. This is a chasing game that some of you may already know.

May I have two volunteers, please? Name yourselves A and B.

A, you are to be a policeman. B, you will be the thief.

The rest of you are to line up in separate, equal rows of five, equally spaced. [They do]

Stretch your arms out from your shoulders. Keep them there.

When I call out "Alleys!" all of you turn a quarter-turn to the right.

When I call "Streets!" turn back to the front.

Remember to keep arms outstretched whatever the call.

Let's practice this a couple of times so that everyone knows how to turn.

They may need to practice a few times so that they all turn together.

Teacher: A and B, move to different parts of the grid so that we can begin the chase along the rows. The rows will change direction when I call "alleys" and change again when I call "streets."

Remember, you can't crash through a blockade of arms or cut through a street or alley. When A tags B, the game is over.

Other students may want to have a chance to take over the roles of policeman and thief. The teacher may use a clapping signal to change the position of the grid. The idea is to make the chase fun and exciting. If it's too easy there'll be no tension. When you or the students have had enough,

Teacher: Let's sit down now and think about that game. Besides a police chase, what other real-life experiences does the game remind you of?

You may wish to use the following strategy; however it is possible to proceed without it. It really depends upon the kinds of curriculum activities that you and the students need to explore together.

Option

1a. Reading pictures to find stories   10–15 minutes

Grouping:	**5 groups**
Strategy:	**Storytelling**
Administration:	**Copies of 5 pictures from the text (Rose in bed, her brother crawling through the door; the children at the wasteland; Jack crawling into the tunnel as Rose looks on; blurred Rose running through the forest; last picture in the book: Rose smiling at Jack); "I *knew you'd come*" is written on the blackboard**
Focus:	**To create interest; to work cooperatively; to engage students in their own story outcomes**
<u>Teacher:</u>	Each group has its own picture. Your task is to make up your own story by using the picture as a source. Be prepared to tell the story you have found in the picture. Use the phrase that is written on the black-board to complete your story.
	This is a collaborative story, so be sure to include everyone's ideas.

Note: It is important that the teacher not read aloud the phrase, "I knew you'd come," so that the students can determine the connotation as they use the phrase in their own contexts.

	Each group will choose a storyteller. When it is your turn, the storyteller will show us the picture and tell us your story. [The stories are shared]
	What did you notice about these stories?

Students will choose a variety of genres: mysteries; science fiction; folktales; and adventure. Here is an opportunity for the teacher to talk about how the students' stories fit into literary genres.

2. Reading the story   7-10 minutes

Grouping:	**Whole group**
Strategy:	**Reading aloud (teacher)**
Administration:	**The storybook; stickies to mark stopping points**
Focus:	**To provide the context and begin to deepen engagement**
<u>Teacher:</u>	Now that we have heard the stories of our class, I am going to read you another version of the story. This one is by author Anthony Browne. He is also the illustrator.
	Come and sit closer, where you can see the pictures. Listen carefully and use your imaginations as we enter the story.

OR

if you have omitted the Option,

<u>Teacher:</u>	Let's begin to explore the story in which this game will, perhaps, play a part. The story is called *The Tunnel* and it is written and illustrated by Anthony Browne.
<u>Teacher reads from</u> <u>beginning to:</u>	*. . . and be back in time for lunch.*

3. Exploring the characters   3 minutes

Grouping:	**Pairs**
Strategy:	**Improvisation**
Administration:	**Space for each pair to work independently**
Focus:	**To find that first sense of the relationship between the brother and sister**

Teacher:

I wonder what it was that the mother heard them say to each other that made her tell them to go outside and play?

Please find yourself a partner. You are the children in the story.

Decide which one of you will be the brother and who will be the sister. Remember, because this is drama, we can be anyone, girls can be the brother and boys can be the sister.

I'd like you to improvise the conversation that your mother overheard just before she sent you outside to play.

First, you need to decide what you two were doing together that caused the problem. [They confer]

Before they start their improvisation, it's a good idea to hear from three or four pairs where their scenes will take place, so that others may be inspired.

Teacher:

Everyone ready to improvise? [They improvise]

You need only give them a minute or so for the improvisation; they probably won't need much practice in arguing!

Teacher:

Talk to your partner about how true to life your improvisation was. Sometimes in drama we tend to exaggerate, and that keeps it from being real. Did you find that you were exaggerating the argument and it wasn't very real? [They talk]

Can anyone suggest ways in which we can make our improvising more real? [They talk]

You might want to take the opportunity for them to redo the scene.

Teacher:

What might be the cause of your arguing so much? [They offer suggestions]

Let's see what else we can find out about this brother and sister.

4. Story reading   1 minute

Grouping:	**Whole group**
Strategy:	**Reading aloud (teacher)**
Administration:	**The storybook**
Focus:	**To build on the improvised argument; to reinforce the perceptions of the brother and sister**

Teacher continues
to read from:

But the boy didn't want his little sister with him to *He went off to explore.*

5. Defining the personalities of the children from what we know   7 *minutes*

Grouping:	**Whole group**
Strategy:	**Role on the wall**
Administration:	**Two life-size cutouts of the boy and the girl laid out on the floor; masking tape or tack gum for the outlines; *red* felt markers for the sister, *blue* felt markers for the brother**
Focus:	**To synthesize our perceptions of the children in the story through the use of adjectives**

Teacher:

I wonder what we would say about these children if we were asked to describe them. What words would you use for the sister? What words would you use for the brother?

If you think you have an idea for an adjective that will describe one or the other of them, come and write those words on the outline to which your adjective applies.

You may write on both outlines and you may feel that you want to use the same word on both outlines. If you do, be sure to use the appropriate colored pen: *red* pen for the sister and *blue* pen for the brother.

Let's start by hearing from someone who has an adjective for the sister. [Someone offers]

Thank you, please come and write your word on this outline.

Right. Let's begin.

Let students add the adjectives and, depending on the class, you may want to comment. Students will comment and talk together as the activity goes on. When you notice that ideas are beginning to slow, you may want to say, "We are about ready to finish up."

Teacher:

While I read these words that you have written, listen and hear how our understanding of these children has grown.

Teacher reads the words as written.

Teacher:

I will now just hang up these two outlines for us to use as a reminder as our story unfolds.

6. Reading for foreshadowing   *1 minute*

Grouping:	**Whole group**
Strategy:	**Reading aloud (teacher)**
Administration:	**The storybook**
Focus:	**To heighten the tension**

Teacher continues
reading from:

Hey, come here to . . . *she began to run faster and faster.*

Grouping:	**Whole group**
Strategies:	**Movement; soundscape**
Administration:	**Overhead projector for lighting; colored lighting gel to enhance atmosphere (red or green); reduce light in room if possible; music (suggested: Vaughan Williams' Symphony No. 7 "Sinfonia Antartica"— Landscape, or other eerie music)**
Focus:	**To create the atmosphere; to permit ourselves to scare and be scared**

Teacher: Our next task is going to be very challenging. You will have to focus and use your imaginations if we want to make our drama work. I wonder if we can become that scary forest?

Note: You will want to work with the whole class first so that they have a kinesthetic understanding of the frightening nature of the woods.

Teacher: Can we create those twisty and scary woods? Let's become the forest that the sister moves through.

                             Find a space in the room where you can stretch your arms without actually touching anyone else. [They do]

                             Listen to the music and allow your body to turn itself into a part of the dark and terrifying forest. [They try this out]

You may need to play the music a couple of times until the students get a sense of the grotesque and frightening nature of the forest.

Teacher: How might we deepen the fearful quality of the woods?

                             Now that we know what these woods look like, I wonder if we can create the sounds of that awful wood? How can we create the scariest place we know? What sorts of sounds would we hear? [They practice adding their sounds to the movement]

                             Who is brave enough to take on the role of the sister? [Someone volunteers]

                             Along with the sounds of the forest, might the sister feel something brushing up against her, catching her clothing, touching her hair but never holding her back? Just think about that.

                             Where will she enter the forest? [They decide]

                             Sister, when you find your way out of the forest, freeze.

                             Trees, when you see her freeze, you freeze as well.

After the students decide where the sister will begin, the whole scene is replayed with movement, sound, and music. Give the students a chance to enjoy the tension and the pleasure of fear. They may want to redo it. If so, choose another student to be the sister. Remember, in drama, it is wise never to do anything over again in exactly the same way.

When the scene freezes (for the last time),

<u>Teacher reads:</u>	*Just when she knew she could run no further, she came to a clearing. [She stopped.] There was a figure, still as stone. It was her brother. "Oh, no!" she sobbed. "I'm too late."*

Option: You or your students may suggest that more than one sister at a time move through the woods. This will depend on the size of your class, their interest, and their ability to build and maintain the tension.

<u>Teacher:</u>	Thank you. Now, find a partner.

8. Creating the brother   *5 minutes*

Grouping:	**Pairs**
Strategy:	**Improvisation**
Administration:	**None**
Focus:	**To persuade**

<u>Teacher:</u>	Decide who is A and who is B.
	As, will you stand for a moment?
	Bs, please sit down.
	(To As) You are the brother who is standing in the clearing still as stone. Can you think to yourself what has happened to make you "as still as stone"?
	As you are thinking about how this happened to you, please go and find a place in the room and create the frozen position that your sister will encounter as she comes into the clearing.
	Remember, you will have to hold this position for quite some time, so make sure that you find a position that you can hold "still as stone."

When the As have found their places,

<u>Teacher:</u>	Relax for a moment and listen.
	Bs, you are now the sister who sees your brother frozen "still as stone" in the clearing. Just think for a moment. How will you break the spell? Will it be your words or your touch that will bring him back to life? Choose your words carefully. Be gentle with your touch. You hold his life in your hands.
	As, think about what your sister might say or do that will break the spell. How will the warmth of her touch or the power of her words restore you to life? In a moment, your sister is going to come and find you. When you feel that your sister's presence has broken the spell, you will say, "I knew you'd come."
	As, take your frozen position "still as stone."

Bs: move slowly toward your partner and when you are ready, begin the scene. When the spell has been broken, sit down quietly together. Don't talk, just wait until everyone is finished.

When the majority of the class is sitting,

Teacher: Thank you, everyone.

9. Storytelling to a partner   *3 minutes*

Grouping: **Pairs (as arranged in previous activity)**
Strategy: **Improvisation**
Administration: **None**
Focus: **To tell a story and retell it**

Teacher: Brothers, tell your sisters the story of what happened to you after you came through the tunnel. [They do]

Who heard a story that you would like to share with the group?

Hear two or three stories. If there is considerable interest, you might want to return to their stories after the drama is completed to have them write them in their pairs. Because the story involves a mysterious occurrence, the students should decide for themselves whether to write the story in the first person or as a narrative.

Teacher: Oh, those were some adventures! I wonder how the brother's story would be different if he were telling it to his mother or a friend?

10. Story reading   *1 minute*

Grouping: **Whole group**
Strategy: **Reading aloud (teacher)**
Administration: **The storybook**
Focus: **To hear the author's version of what the sister did**

Teacher: Now let's hear Anthony Browne's story of how the brother was brought back to life.

If the stories you have heard are similar to Browne's, you may want to add, "You will probably find that you and he are not too far apart in how the story is unfolding."

Teacher reads from: *"Oh, no," she sobbed. "I'm too late,"* to the end of the story.

11. Reflecting in role

Grouping:	**Whole group working individually**
Strategy:	**Writing in role**
Administration:	**Paper and pencils**
Focus:	**To debrief the experience for themselves in role**

Teacher: Quietly, take a piece of paper and a pencil and find your own space and sit down.

I'd like you to imagine that you are either Jack or Rose. It is now bed-time and you have been thinking about your experience all day. You are sitting in your bedroom, writing in your diary about what happened.

Take out your diary and begin to write about the day's experience. What will you say? What have you learned about yourself? Will you write about your fears, your courage, your brother or sister? What is it about the day that you will record?

Let the students write for three to five minutes, depending on their writing skills. Note: Don't worry if you see them stop for a while. They may be thinking, and if you don't rush them, they may start to write again.

Teacher: Read over what you have written and choose the sentence that you think best reflects your thinking and feeling. Underline that sentence and memorize it.

An example of writing in role as Jack: "My sister is not such a sissy. I never thought she'd ever in a million years crawl through the tunnel. She's afraid of the dark—she sleeps with a night-light. But she did it. I know she was scared, she always is—but she kept going. She was worried about me. She even told me she loves me. I never told her back that I love her, too."

12. Collective sharing of experience

Grouping:	**Whole group**
Strategy:	**Tapping in**
Administration:	**Student writing**
Focus:	**To reflect**

Teacher: When you feel my hand on your shoulder, we will hear your words. Speak so that we can all hear you and share your thoughts. When you have finished, put your head down so that I know you have spoken.

The teacher moves randomly through the room, placing a hand (quite firmly) on a student's shoulder. Note: Leave your hand there until the student has finished speaking, then move on. After each student has contributed, ask,

Teacher: Before you fall asleep, is there anything else you want to say to each other? [They may add]

Good night, Rose.

Good night, Jack. I love you.

13. Rounding out the characters of Jack and Rose   3–4 minutes

Grouping:	**Whole group**
Strategy:	**Role on the wall**
Administration:	**Pens of different colors (note: no red or blue pens); cutouts of the children hanging on the wall**
Focus:	**To discover a change in perspective through reflection**

Teacher: Let's look at Rose and Jack again.

Knowing what we know now, what new words or adjectives do we want to add to the children? How have our ideas about them changed and grown?

You may choose a pen in any color.

14. Whole-class reflection on the drama experience   as needed

Grouping:	**Whole group**
Strategy:	**Reflection**
Administration:	**None**
Focus:	**To relate the drama experience to the students' lives**

Teacher: What sorts of things might make you change your feelings and thoughts about someone or something?

In what other stories that we know do people go through some kind of obstacle or test (like the tunnel that Jack and Rose go through)? What is it about being able to overcome something that makes a story really powerful?

I wonder if you noticed that the author, Anthony Browne, doesn't refer to the children by name until right near the end of the story? Why do you think he did that?

Let's talk about our drama. Which activities helped you to create the drama world? Talk to the people next to you about that before we share.

If applicable:

Teacher: You remember the experience in the scary forest? I wonder why we wanted to play the forest scene over again? What is it about scaring or being scared that is so much fun?

I wonder if you could see the game that we played at the beginning of class in the experience of Rose in the forest?

Note: The first three questions are learning integrators, using the thoughts and feelings experienced in the drama to relate to wider issues in the students' lives. The last three reflection questions draw the students' attention to the ways in which the drama was made.

Resource

Browne, A. 1992. *The Tunnel*. London: Walker Books.

Materials

We assume that you will have a chalkboard and chalk available.

Optional Activity 1a:	Illustrations from the book: 1. Rose in bed, her brother crawling through the door; 2. The children at the wasteland; 3. Jack crawling into the tunnel as Rose looks on; 4. Last picture in the book: Rose smiling at Jack; "I knew you'd come" written on chalkboard or chart paper.
Activity 2:	A copy of the story, with stickies to mark the stopping points.
Activity 4.	Storybook
Activity 5:	2 cutouts; masking tape or tack gum; red and blue felt markers
Activity 6:	Storybook
Activity 7:	Overhead projector; colored lighting gels; music
Activity 10:	Storybook
Activity 11:	Paper and pencils
Activity 12:	Student writing
Activity 13:	Outline of children; multiple colored pens (no red or blue)

The Tunnel
Cross-Curricular Extension

This extension is offered for those who are interested in following up on *The Tunnel,* or those who need to examine the problems of bullying or sibling rivalry. It works very well with older students but can be done with students of any age. It is designed to follow the story drama outlined above, on another day.

Grouping:	**Whole group**
Strategy:	**Teacher in role as facilitator; students in role as parents**
Administration:	**Chairs in a circle; table (optional)**
Focus:	**To extend and apply understandings developed in The Tunnel**

Teacher:	In a moment, we are all going to go into role and I will be playing a part in the drama with you.
	I want you to listen really carefully so that you can find out who you are and who I am. I think it will be clear to you but if, at any time, things are not clear, all you have to do is put up your hand and say, "Out of role," and we will stop the drama and clear up the difficulty. Is that clear?
	Let's put the chairs in a circle.

You might like to have a table to sit around; it depends upon the size of your class.

Teacher:	Please stand behind your chair. We will be in role when we sit down. Everyone clear? Good. Off we go!
Teacher in role as principal:	(*To the parents*) It's wonderful to see so many parents who are able to be here this evening. Please sit down. [They do]
	I do want to thank you for coming out this evening. As principal of Northwood, I am honored that you all think there is something that we can do here to help you find ways to help your children.
	I gather from a number of you with whom I have been speaking that you are concerned about your children's behavior at home—primarily, with their attitudes and behavior toward each other. I appreciate very much your understanding that poor behavior at home can affect behavior in school and, of course, the other way around.
	My teachers and I are anxious to work together with you. Only in this way can we truly effect change.
	There seem to be a number of issues about your children's behavior that are concerning you. We might begin by addressing these tonight.
Teacher out of role:	What seems to be happening here?

It is helpful to check in with your students at this point just to make sure that they all understand the rules so far. For example:

- Do you know who you are? Who I am?
- Do you understand what the problem is?

Teacher:	Good. Are we ready to go on?

2. Building the information they need to work with *5 minutes*

Grouping:	**Groups of 3 or 4**
Strategy:	**Building lists**
Administration:	**Black felt pens (1 per group); large sheets of paper (1 per group); new space for group work (leave chairs in circle)**
Focus:	**To create the concerns by drawing upon the previous experience**

Teacher: Would you please go into groups of no more than three or four?

For this next task, you will need to think as if you were parents. Even though you are not in role, you will be thinking the way parents would think.

Use the pens and paper and build a list of three to five concerns about children's behavior that parents might have. [They work for three to five minutes]

3. Building collective concerns *5–6 minutes*

Grouping:	**Whole group**
Strategy:	**Building lists**
Administration:	**Chalk and chalkboard or flowchart paper; black felt pen**
Focus:	**To synthesize a list of collective concerns**

Teacher: Let's see what we have. We'll hear from each group in turn. Just give us one idea from your list.

If any other group has that idea on their list, just put a tick beside it so we don't have repetitions.

Teacher records each group's contribution.

Teacher: Does that seem to cover it all? Good.

This list will be important to us in the next part of our drama.

Tidy up the pens and paper. Return to your chairs and stand behind them. [They do]

You will need to listen carefully again, because we will be going into role, but our roles will change.

4. Meeting as counselors and psychologists *5 minutes*

Grouping:	**Whole group**
Strategies:	**Teacher in role; Mantle of the expert**
Administration:	**Circle of chairs; table (optional)**
Focus:	**To set about solving the concerns of the parents**

Teacher in role as facilitator: Good afternoon, ladies and gentlemen. Please sit down.

There has been, as you know, a great deal of concern on the part of the parents in our schools about sibling rivalry. Of course, many parents are now having to function as single parents and that can also add to their concerns, but I believe it goes deeper than that. However, I am not the expert here; you are.

I have been asked by the school board to bring our district school counselors together to see if we can come up with a brochure that would be of help to parents who are having difficulties.

I welcome you all and thank you for making your time available for this task.

Perhaps you would like to identify yourselves and tell us what school you serve in and how long you have been a counselor. In such a large and busy district as ours, I doubt that many of us know each other. [They do]

The principal of Northwood has provided us with a list of concerns that the parents have expressed. I think it best if we get directly down to business. We have made a master list which you see here. As you study it, please feel free to share your own experience or any suggestions or advice you may have in response to the issues identified on this list.

As the students respond, you need to listen, question, and clarify (by pressing for explanation) the experiences that led to their knowledge. For example:

- You have had an incident like that in your school?
- How effective did you find that solution?
- Were the children able to offer any ideas to solve the problem?
- What part does the parent play in all this?

When you feel that there is enough information to help them and that there is sufficient engagement and investment in the situation, you can move on. While there may be opportunities for further improvisation, role-play, and dramatic exploration through any number of strategies, what we suggest extends the application of the lesson into other disciplines. The students may continue to work in role or to work out of role.

Suggested Activities for Cross-Curricular Integration

Research:
Boys and Girls Club
Buddy programs on the playground/
Peer counseling programs
Help lines
Social Service agencies

Designing:
Brochures
Posters
A bedroom for siblings that provides space
for individual as well as shared activities
(looking at square footage, spatial dimensions, human measurements, air and light
requirements, colors, etc.)

Writing:
Letters to the editor
Brochure text
Class questionnaire on sibling habits

Planning:
After-school programs and activities

Presenting:
Inviting the principal/parents/ counseling
staff et cetera to a display and presentation of
research

Resources

For more information on teacher in role and mantle of the expert:

Heathcote, D., and G. Bolton. 1995. *Drama for Learning: Dorothy Heathcote's Mantle of the Expert Approach to Education*. Portsmouth, NH:
Heinemann.

Morgan, N., and J. Saxton. 1987. *Teaching Drama: A mind of many wonders*. Cheltenham, UK: Stanley Thornes. (Chapter 3: Teaching in
Role)

Suggested Stories and Books

Sibling Rivalry

Blume, Judy. 1984. *The Pain and the Great One*. New York: Simon &
Schuster.

Curtis, Christopher Paul. 1995. *The Watsons Go to Birmingham*. New
York: Delacorte.

Ephron, Delia. 1993. *The Girl Who Changed the World*. London: Ticknor
& Fields.

Joose, Barbara. 1988. *Anna, the One and Only*. New York: Harper.

Park, Barbara. 1982. *Operation: Dump the Chump*. New York: Knopf.

Yorinks, Arthur. 1989. *Oh, Brother*. New York: Farrar.

Brothers and Sisters
Byars, Betsy. 1986. *Not-Just-Anybody Family*. New York: Delacorte.

Clymer, Eleanor. 1989. *My Brother Stevie*. New York: Dell.

Delton, Judy. 1995. *Angel in Charge*. New York: Houghton Mifflin.

Greenwald, Sheila. 1989. *The Atrocious Two*. New York: Dell.

Little, Jean. 1965. *Far from Home*. New York: Little, Brown.

MacLachlan, Patricia. 1991. *Journey*. New York: Delacorte.

Skurzynski, Gloria. 1988. *The Minstrel in the Tower*. New York: Random House.

CHAPTER SIX

Racing Northward

Based on *The Polar Express*
written and illustrated by Chris Van Allsburg

Why Did We Choose This Story?

■ *The Polar Express* has become one of the most popular stories celebrating the Christmas season. It is secular and is therefore appropriate for today's diverse classrooms.

■ In times when materialism has become more important than the essence of the holiday, the story brings our perspective back to what is truly important.

■ The story is told from the perspective of a child and evokes that childlike joy that is sometimes lost in the frenzy of the holiday time.

■ The language and the imagery of the language are present in the illustrations and the illustrations themselves would stand alone as stimuli for descriptive writing.

■ The themes reflect our ideas of growing up and the importance of remembering that what is mysterious can yet, in some strange way, be perfectly believable.

Key Understandings and Questions

■ Why is it that as we grow older we lose our ability to fantasize?
■ Often the simplest thing contains the greatest history.
■ What is the true meaning of the word *gift*?

1. Introducing the story   *5 minutes*

Grouping:	**Whole group**
Strategy:	**Predicting**
Administration:	**Holiday items—tin of cocoa; a piece of greenery from a fir tree; a little gift box; a jingle bell or harmony ball (something with a delicate sound/ring)**
Focus:	**To create interest**

Teacher arranges holiday items on a table or chair in front of the students.

Teacher:	I wonder what sort of story might have these objects in it? [They share ideas]

2. Context setting   *3 minutes*

Grouping:	**Whole class**
Strategy:	**Discussion**
Administration:	**None**
Focus:	**To foreshadow**

Teacher:	Who has ever lost something that was very precious to them?
	When you think about the thing you have lost, what do you remember? What regrets might you have about losing it?
	Share your thoughts with a partner.

If appropriate:

Teacher:	Anybody have something they'd like to share?
	Where might those things that get lost end up, I wonder?

3. Precious gifts   *10 minutes*

Grouping:	**Whole group**
Strategy:	**Game**
Administration:	**None**
Focus:	**To engage with the story**

Teacher:	We know that the season we are in now is called winter. Not only do we see changes in the weather, in our gardens, in our house, and what we wear, but we also see changes in the stores.
	Anyone been shopping with their parents lately? What sort of changes do you see in the stores? [Lots of gift items, decorations, music, and so on]
	The story we are working with today takes place in this holiday season. Even though this story is about Christmas, we know that there are many other holidays celebrated at this time of year. Each one is about bringing warmth and light and joy to family and friends.

Often we exchange gifts and the person responsible for presents for many children is a big, jolly man in a red suit called Santa Claus.

It is likely that you will not have to tell them this name because they will already be telling you.

Teacher:

To get ready for our drama, we are going to play a game that's about gift giving but before we can give a gift away, we have to have one. And because this is drama, we can imagine those gifts.

Think of something that you treasure and that you would be prepared to give away. It must be something that you can hold in your hand and that will give happiness to the receiver.

Take a moment to think about what it is that you would be prepared to give away.

Imagine you are holding this special treasure in your hands now.

Look across the room and find someone with whom to exchange gifts.

Everyone found someone? Good.

In a moment, you are going to cross to that person you have found. Tell your partner what your gift to them is and they will do the same to you.

Some examples: "This is my mom's ring"; "This is my teddy bear that I've had since I was a baby . . ."

Teacher:

When you have exchanged gifts, you now have your partner's gift to give away. Remember it is precious, so treat it carefully and be sure that the person you give it to knows exactly what it is.

Teacher may wish to demonstrate two exchanges to be sure that students understand.

Teacher:

Are we ready? Right, off you go.

Let the game continue for about seven exchanges.

Teacher:

Stop now and don't let go of the gift you have just received. Make sure that you know what it is.

Return to your seat.

Well, let's hear what everyone is holding.

Teacher does a whole-class-circle checkup. There may be some gifts missing and/or some gifts may appear twice or more.

Teacher:

What do you think might have happened to those gifts that were lost? [Students offer suggestions]

Teacher:

Our story is about a special and precious gift that was received by a young boy at Christmas. It is a very special story that some of you may know. *The Polar Express* by Chris Van Allsburg won the Caldecott Medal as the best book of the year for children.

4. Entering the story

3 minutes

Grouping:	**Whole group**
Strategy:	**Reading aloud (teacher)**
Administration:	**The storybook, with a stickie to mark the end of the first reading**
Focus:	**To listen**

Teacher shows the cover of the book to the students.

<u>Teacher:</u> The *Polar Express* is the name of the train. I wonder why you think it is called the *Polar Express*. Why would a train be named that?

Note: Some children may never have seen or heard a train or know the meaning of "express," so it is important to be sure that the context is clear for all your students.

<u>Teacher reads to the end of the second page of the text:</u> *. . . and he pulled me aboard.*

5. Creating the train

10 minutes

Grouping:	**Whole group in a large empty space, perhaps the front of your room**
Strategies:	**Soundscape; dramatic play; teacher in role**
Administration:	**The storybook; a whistle on a chain or a uniform cap for the conductor**
Focus:	**To create a train in which we can all believe**

Teacher shows class picture of trains on back cover.

<u>Teacher:</u> How many carriages might there be on a train called the *Polar Express*? I can only see two carriages and an engine. [They offer]

I wonder what a carriage on the *Polar Express* would look like inside. Let's create the inside of the train car, just using our own bodies.

Students may use chairs or sit on the floor to make the carriage. Whatever they do, go with it even if it is not exactly correct or, if it matters to you, show them some pictures of the inside of train carriages.

<u>Teacher:</u> So now that we've made our train, I wonder what sounds we would hear if we were inside the train carriage? What sounds do you remember hearing about in the story?

Some examples: the hiss of the steam, squeaking of metal.

Let's close our eyes and imagine the sounds that we might hear as we are riding north. Listen to the sounds in your mind's ear.

Now, begin to make those sounds out loud. [They do]

Good! Now we have the soundscape and the setting; there is just one more thing we need to make sure that our journey is comfortable—a conductor!

Perhaps there is a child who has been on a train and can talk about the conductor.

<u>Teacher:</u> Just as every classroom has a teacher, every train car has a conductor. The *Polar Express* is no exception.

What might the conductor be doing? What jobs do you think he might have? [They offer—taking tickets, helping people on and off, assisting with luggage, and so on]

Now that we have prepared our scene, we are just about ready to start our journey on the *Polar Express.*

Teacher hangs the whistle around her neck or puts on the cap.

Teacher: When I come aboard the train, I will be in role as your conductor. Are we ready to begin our journey northward? All aboard!

Teacher "boards" and moves through the "car," taking tickets, welcoming passengers, asking if they would like something to drink or eat and putting luggage up on the racks, et cetera.

Teacher circulates among the students, playing at being on the train. You may wish to stop after a few minutes and ask,

Teacher: Do we have it right? Can we really imagine that we are on the train?

Sometimes children will suggest things that need to be improved or could be tried. If so, go with all ideas until everyone is happy. This dramatic play should last about five minutes.

Teacher: Well now, we have certainly been using our imaginations and we are ready to go back to our story.

6. The beginning of the journey   2 minutes

Grouping:	**Whole class**
Strategy:	**Reading aloud (teacher)**
Administration:	**The storybook, with stickies to mark the beginning and end of section**
Focus:	**To find themselves in the story**

Teacher reads from: *"The train was filled"* to *". . . is the North Pole."*

7. Looking out the train window   15 minutes

Grouping:	**Individual**
Strategy:	**Drawing**
Administration:	**Overhead projector transparencies, one for each child; felt pens OR for younger children: sheets of paper (suggested 8½-by-14 inches); felt pens**
Focus:	**To imagine as illustrators beyond the story**

Teacher: If you were illustrating this book, which scene would you choose to draw in order to convey what the children saw as they looked through the windows of the *Polar Express?*

You may wish to have a brief conversation about all the possibilities before moving on to the next task. You may choose to reread certain descriptive phrases as prompts.

Teacher: I will give each of you your own overhead transparency. Use your felts to create the scene that you would have seen from the train. [They do]

8. Imagining the sounds   10 *minutes*

Grouping:	**Groups of 4**
Strategy:	**Decision making**
Administration:	**Students' illustrations; large sheet of unlined chart paper**
Focus:	**To find the picture with the most sound potential**

Teacher: In your groups, share your pictures. Use the large sheet of white paper to lay them on so that you can see them easily. Be careful not to smudge them.

These are wonderful pictures. You are really seeing as illustrators.

Now, I am going to ask you to choose one of these pictures, but this time your choice is going to be made as if you were *sound designers*. Decide together which one picture helps you to imagine the sounds that you would hear if you were inside that picture. [They choose]

9. Bringing the picture to life   5 *minutes*

Grouping:	**Groups of 4**
Strategy:	**Soundscape**
Administration:	**Overhead projector; the selected illustrated transparencies; one percussion instrument per group (optional)**
Focus:	**To work as sound designers**

Teacher: Now that you have chosen the picture, your task is to create the sound-scape using your own voices to accompany the illustration that you have chosen. You may use your percussion instrument if it will be helpful.

Think about those sounds and work them through so that there is a beginning, a middle, and an end. You will need to know how you are going to start it and how you will end it.

You must be able to repeat it so that the sound brings the picture to life.

10. Presenting our sound and scene designs   7 *minutes*

Grouping:	**Groups of 4**
Strategy:	**Soundscape**
Administration:	**Overhead projector; the selected illustrated transparencies; one percussion instrument per group (optional)**
Focus:	**To create a sound background for the picture**

Teacher: Let's decide in which order our groups will present. Which group thinks that they have the picture to begin our journey? [They select]

Which group thinks that they have the final picture? [They select]

Good. Now, who will be second? And third?

Process continues until the order of presentation has been decided.

Teacher:	This is how our presentation will work. I will dim the lights. We will all close our eyes. I will then ask the first group to start their sound-scape. We will listen to it and then we will open our eyes and see the illustration on the overhead projector.
	The group that is presenting needs to continue their soundscape as we look at the picture.
	Then we will close our eyes again. Although the picture will disappear, the soundscape will slowly fade away until there is silence.

Teacher collects the pictures in order, puts them by the overhead projector. Darken the room (if possible). Put the first group's illustration on the projector, ready to be added to the soundscape.

Teacher:	Close your eyes and listen carefully.
	When you hear the overhead switching on, or I tell you, that will be your signal to open your eyes. All right, are everyone's eyes closed?
	Group one: You may begin when you are ready.

Groups present one after the other.

Teacher:	Those were wonderful set and sound designs. Full of atmosphere.
	Talk to your group about what you heard and saw. [They do]
	How did this help to bring the story alive for you? [They discuss]

OR

If you are working with younger students, crayons and paper might be more suitable than transparencies. You could then put the completed scenes up as a freeze around the room. Students may wish to title their illustrations.

11. Arriving at the North Pole   2 minutes

Grouping:	**Whole group**
Strategy:	**Reading aloud (teacher)**
Administration:	**The storybook, with a stickie to mark the beginning and end of the reading**
Focus:	**To hear what happens at the North Pole**

Teacher:	Now we're ready to go on with our story.
Teacher reads from:	*The North Pole. It was a . . .* to *The elves cheered wildly.*
Teacher:	Remember the conductor? We're going to meet him again. Are we ready?

12. Looking into our hearts   3 minutes

Grouping:	**Whole group**
Strategy:	**Teacher in role**
Administration:	**Cap or whistle; chair**
Focus:	**To discover what it is that Santa sees in us**

Teacher puts on cap (or whistle) and sits in chair.

Teacher in role as conductor:	Well, children. It is very difficult for Santa to choose the child who will receive the first gift of Christmas.
	Santa and I have pondered this dilemma for many, many years. I wonder what it is that Santa sees in someone's heart that tells him, "This one."
	Children, maybe you could help me understand how Santa would make such a choice. Help me to understand this. [They offer ideas]

Teacher needs to press students to clarify what they are saying. For example, if a students says, "Someone who is good." You need to ask, "What do you mean by good?" and ask them for examples.

| Teacher: | It will be interesting to see whom Santa chooses this year. |

13. Santa makes a choice   2 minutes

Grouping:	**Whole group**
Strategy:	**Reading aloud (teacher)**
Administration:	**The storybook with a stickie to mark the beginning**
Focus:	**To conclude the story**

| Teacher reads from: | *He marched over to us* to the end of the story |

Option for Younger Students

14a. A letter to Santa   5 minutes

Grouping:	**Pairs**
Strategy:	**Writing in role**
Administration:	**Paper and pencils**
Focus:	**To thank Santa and tell him what happened**

| Upon closing the book, Teacher: | I wonder how we would explain to Santa what happened? |
| | With a partner, you will write your letter to Santa and tell him about what happened on Christmas morning. You might like to thank Santa for returning the lost bell. |

Remember to leave lots of time for the students to talk together and to compose their letters.

OR

Teacher and class could write the letter to Santa together.

14b. Sharing their letters   5 minutes

Grouping:	**Whole group**
Strategy:	**Teacher in role**
Administration:	**Special box for letters; cap or whistle**
Focus:	**To remain inside the story**

Teacher puts on cap (or whistle).

| Teacher in role as conductor: | Children, the *Polar Express* is leaving for the North Pole for the year and won't be back until next Christmas. I understand you have written to Santa about what happened to you on Christmas morning. What did happen? |

This presents the opportunity for the students to share what they have written. One or two might like to read from their letters; others may share orally. No need to hear from everyone.

| Teacher: | Right, then. Fold up your letters and put them in this box and I will be sure that Santa receives them the moment we arrive. |

Teacher collects the letters in a special box. Make sure that the box disappears at the end of the day as a conclusion to the drama.

Option for Older Children

14c. *From generation to generation* **5 minutes**

Grouping:	**Individual**
Strategy:	**Writing in role**
Administration:	**Paper and pencils**
Focus:	**To tell the story of the bell**

Teacher:	I'd like you to imagine that your journey on the *Polar Express* took place forty years ago and you have never forgotten it.
	Your child is now the same age as you were when you received the bell from Santa.
	This is the Christmas that you will give him the bell. You will pass the bell on to him.
	Write the letter that will accompany the gift. Remember, you are writing in role as the boy grown up. You are now a father and this is the story of what happened to you many years ago.
	What will you tell him about the bell?
	How will you describe what happened when you opened the gift?
	Later, your letter will be opened and read by your child.

The children write. Be sure to give them at least four to five minutes and don't be worried if they stop writing for a while. In our experience, they are thinking hard.

| Teacher: | Finish the sentence you are working on. Read over what you have written. Take a moment to add anything or make any changes. When you are ready, fold up your letter and put your initials on it. Bring it to the center of the room and put it here. |

The initials prevent you from giving a student his or her own letter back. When all the students have placed their letters in the center, teacher gives each student a different letter to read.

| Teacher: | I'm going to ask you to switch roles now. When you read the letter, you are to read in role as the child. This is the story of what happened to your father many years ago. |

Open your letter and begin reading. [They do]

Out of role now. What sentences made the story come alive for you?

Let's hear some of those. [They read those sentences aloud to everyone]

Even though the story of the bell was the same, how we tell that story says something about each one of us. Thank you.

15. Reflection   *as needed*

Grouping:	**Whole group**
Strategy:	**Discussion**
Administration:	**None**
Focus:	**To generate thinking beyond the story; to look at the themes underlying the story**

Use as many of these questions as you wish to explore with your students.

Teacher:

Why was it, do you think, that the children could hear the bell and their parents could not?

Why do you think that the boy was able to hear the bell all his life?

For the boy in our story, the silver bell was the first Christmas gift of that year. Imagine that you could take the *Polar Express* this year and that *you* are the child that Santa chooses to ask for the first gift. What would you ask for?

What would be special to you about this first Christmas gift?

You know, one of the things about this story that really interests me is why those children who are only wearing their pajamas and slippers aren't cold. The elves, too, aren't wearing a lot of clothes. Does anyone have any ideas about why no one is cold?

Suggested Extensions

The activities that follow are not sequential.

For Readers
Story mapping
- In groups of 4.
- Each group has a copy of the words of the text (no illustrations).
- A large sheet of craft paper and felts.
- Task: to create a story map of the events in the story.

For Nonreaders
Story mapping on the board with the teacher
- Story-map as a class, with teacher listing the events.
OR
- Students offer ideas about pictorial symbols that could help them recall the sequence of events.

For Readers
Retelling
- Groups of 4, numbered 1–4.
- Task: to tell the story of *The Polar Express*. Number 1 begins.
- When teacher says "Change," number 2 will continue and so on until all groups are finished.

For Readers
Perspective-taking
Retell the story using "change" as before.
- 1s as if they were the conductor
- 2s as if they were a parent of the boy in the story
- 3s as if they were an elf
- 4s as if they were the boy now a father himself, telling his son about the events of that night so long ago

Retelling
Easy version using the story map
- Who would like to begin retelling our story?
- Let's look at our story map to see where the story begins.

Students continue volunteering, using the story map as a guide. Teacher encourages as many students as possible to contribute.

Retelling
Complex version using the story map
- I wonder how the story would change if another character in the story were telling it?
- Let's think about who else could tell a part of the story. [They do]

■ Which of the events on our story map could that person tell? [They decide]

Suggested Other Activities

1. Retell the story as if you were a reporter. Be sure to identify the kind of magazine or newspaper that you work for, to be able to write from the appropriate "angle."
2. Map the route from where you live to the North Pole. What sorts of things might you see? What adventure might you have on your way to the North Pole?
3. Check with a travel agent about getting to the North Pole. How close could you get by conventional transportation? What other ways could you travel there? How much would it cost? What kinds of clothes should you take? What other questions can you think of to ask?

Resources

Van Allsburg, C. 1985. *The Polar Express*. NY: Houghton Mifflin. *www.eduplace.com/tview/tviews/p/polarexpress.html/*

Materials

Activity 1:	Tin of cocoa; a piece of greenery from a fir tree; a little gift box; jingle bell or harmony ball (something with a delicate sound/ring)
Activity 4:	The storybook, with a stickie to mark the end of the first reading
Activity 5:	A whistle on a chain or a uniform cap for the conductor
Activity 6:	The storybook, with a stickie to mark the beginning and end of the reading
Activity 7:	Overhead projector transparencies, one for each child; felt pens
	OR for younger children: sheets of paper (suggested sizes, 8½-by-14 inches); felt pens
Activity 8:	Students' illustrations; large sheet of unlined chart paper
Activities 9 and 10:	Overhead projector; the selected illustrated transparencies Optional: one percussion instrument per group
Activity 11:	The storybook, with a stickie to mark the beginning and end of the reading
Activity 12:	Cap or whistle; chair
Activity 13:	The storybook with a stickie to mark the beginning and end of the reading
Activity 14a:	Paper and pencils
Activity 14b:	Special box for letters
Activity 14c:	Paper and pencils

CHAPTER SEVEN

Of Dark and Wolfish Things

Based on *The Werewolf Knight*
written by Jenny Wagner and illustrated by Robert Roennfeldt

Why Did We Choose This Story?

■ It is a story with wide appeal, as the idea of transformation is one that is present in much of our literature.

■ The structure is one that works across any number of grade levels.

■ The text uses simple language that evokes our deepest responses.

■ At a time when the *Harry Potter* stories have captured the imaginations of children and adults around the world, *The Werewolf Knight* capitalizes on students' knowledge of the magic of story.

■ While the story can be used at any time throughout the year, Of Dark and Wolfish Things will meet the needs of those who are looking for a new addition to the canon of Halloween stories.

Key Understandings and Questions

■ We often make assumptions about people before we really know them.
■ How many times have we taken advice without considering where it comes from or whom it may affect?
■ How do our own personal interests affect how we relate to others?

1. Setting the context   *5 minutes*

Grouping:	**Whole group**
Strategy:	**Reading a picture**
Administration:	**Overhead projector; overhead of the picture of the wedding guests at court (left page only)**
Focus:	**To introduce the context of the story**
<u>Teacher:</u>	What do you see in this picture that might tell us something about the story we are going to enter?

Optional Entry Point

1a. Setting the context   *5 minutes*

Grouping:	**Whole group**
Strategy:	**Reading artifacts**
Administration:	**A table covered with a large piece of "royal" fabric on which a variety of artifacts that relate to the focus of the story and which signal medieval times are placed. Some examples: a piece of fur; a sheet of parchment or a copy of a page of illustrated manuscript; a small dagger or a long sword; a goblet; a cloak; candle stick with a burnt-down candle; a quill pen**
Focus:	**To introduce the context of the story**
<u>Teacher:</u>	Let's walk around this exhibit of artifacts and think about what you see that might tell us something about the story we are about to enter?

We are looking for the children to identify the fact that this story takes place long ago; that it has to do with some kind of formal environment.

<u>Teacher:</u>   The interesting thing about this story is that it has been around for a very long time and like many old stories, it has gone through many changes.

Optional if appropriate:

<u>Teacher:</u>   This time of the year is a time of change. We can see nature transforming itself. What have you been noticing about the changes in nature? [They offer]

All of those changes often have an effect on us, on how we feel and how we act. I know that when it gets cold and dark, I slow down just like the bears, almost as if I were getting ready to hibernate.

2. Impressions of werewolves   5 minutes

Grouping:	**Whole group**
Strategy:	**Brainstorming**
Administration:	**Chart paper, felt pen**
Focus:	**To draw out shared understandings about werewolves**

Teacher: Today's drama has a lot to do with transformation and change. Around this time of year (Halloween), we hear quite a lot about the werewolf. What are some of the things we've heard about werewolves?

Let's hear some of our ideas and I will write them down. [Students offer and teacher scribes]

Let's keep this list for our reference. It's going to help us with what we do next.

3. Transforming into a werewolf   5 minutes

Grouping:	**Pairs**
Strategy:	**Sculpting or molding**
Administration:	**Pairs work in their own spaces**
Focus:	**To translate ideas kinesthetically**

Teacher: Find a partner and a space on your own. Sit down together.

Decide who is A and who is B.

As, you are going to be a sculptor. Using the ideas that we listed, you are going to "sculpt" your partner into a werewolf.

Bs, you are going to be a piece of clay that will be transformed by the sculptor into a werewolf. Now, as clay, remember that you can't speak, and you must be soft and malleable so that the sculptor can create his vision of the werewolf on you.

Sculptors, remember to be very gentle with your clay. Do not put your partner into a position that will be hard to hold.

When we are finished, this room will be transformed into a huge exhibit of statues of werewolves.

Have the students work quickly to produce the "exhibit," about ninety seconds.

Teacher: Everyone, thirty seconds until the exhibit opens.

Freeze, everyone.

Werewolves, your challenge now is to remain frozen. This is going to be hard and you will need to concentrate on maintaining your position. You will also need to remember how it feels for another activity later on.

Sculptors, leave your statue and stand by the wall. Be sure to stand where you can see most statues.

What do you notice about these werewolves? What do you see? [They tell] Thank you.

Werewolves, relax. That was hard! But we have a good idea about what a werewolf looks like and lots of ideas about their dispositions. Some of you were very frightening.

Just sit down with your partner for a moment.

4. Becoming the knight   5 minutes

Grouping:	**As in Activity 3**
Strategy:	**Sculpting or molding**
Administration:	**Tambourine**
Focus:	**To translate the ideas kinesthetically**

Teacher: The title of our story is *The Werewolf Knight*. When I first heard this title, I thought it would be a story about werewolves doing something scary at night. But when I saw the cover and read the title, I realized that this was about a different kind of "knight"—a medieval knight.

What are some of the things we know about medieval knights?

Let's hear some of our ideas.

Students' remarks should build on ideas of nobility, honor, chivalry, and so on. Teacher may scribe as before or not, as is appropriate to the group.

Teacher: Bs, you are going to sculpt your piece of clay into a knight as he is performing some kind of heroic deed. Think about what that deed might be. Don't tell your piece of clay but mold it in such a way that it will know the story of the deed.

As, as clay, remember the instructions your partner received before? Remain malleable and easy to shape; no talking.

Again, you will not have much time, so get to work and work quickly; quickly but carefully. Remember, there is a code of knightly conduct that this statue will represent.

The students work for about 90 seconds.

Teacher: Thirty seconds, everyone.

It is useful to give students warning when time is almost up. It spurs the slow ones on and allows those who are done to know that they have a little time to make things better.

Teacher: Freeze. Sculptors, take one step away from your statue and see what you have created. Look around from where you are to see the other knight statues. Where do you see the knightly qualities we spoke of? [They share]

Relax, everyone, and listen very carefully.

Now is the hard part. I am going to ask you to do something that you have not had a chance to practice, although you know how to do it already. Are you ready?

Face your partner. Close your eyes.

Knights, take your statue positions.

Werewolves, take your statue positions.

Everyone, open your eyes. Look carefully at your partner. Focus. This is difficult work. Hold your pose and listen to my instructions.

As you hear the five beats on the tambourine, in slow motion, you will begin to transform yourself into the other: knights becoming werewolves; werewolves becoming knights. This takes tremendous control and it lies at the heart of our story.

By the fifth beat, you will have completed your transformation. [They move to five slow beats]

Freeze. Well done! Would you like the chance to transform back again?

Most students will want to participate. Those who choose not to transform back may sit where they are and observe.

Teacher:	Hold your positions and stand by to transform. [They move as before to the five slow beats]
Teacher:	Just talk to your partner about that experience. [They do]
	Who has something they would like to share? [They share]

Students will have a variety of responses. This debriefing is important to release some of the energy of the moment.

5. The story begins   2 minutes

Grouping:	**Whole group**
Strategy:	**Reading aloud (teacher)**
Administration:	**The storybook**
Focus:	**To enter the story**

| Teacher: | I think we are ready for our story now. Just sit down where you are and be ready to listen. |
| | Unlike most fairy tales that you know already, the characters in this story have true medieval names. The knight's name is Feolf and the princess's name is Fioran. |

Teacher may want to write these names on the board or on chart paper.

| Teacher reads: | *Feolf was a knight to . . . and she dreaded marrying him.* |
| Teacher continues: | *On the eve of the wedding, she went to her father's court magician[s] and asked [them] what she should do.* |

Note: In the sentence above, the text has been changed to the plural.

6. Being magicians

Grouping:	**Groups of 4 or 5**
Strategy:	**Dramatic play**
Administration:	**None; students may choose to use some representational props**
Focus:	**To build belief**

Teacher:

The king believed in looking after his people and so there were many magicians in this court with many different skills. These magicians worked very hard.

What sorts of things might these magicians do? [They offer]

In groups of four or five, decide what kinds of work you might do as court magicians. In a moment, when we continue our drama, we will see all of the court magicians busy at work.

Take a moment to decide together what you would be doing and where you would be doing it. Shall we say that it is late evening? You decide if you need to talk as you are working. It is important for us to discover what it is that these magicians are skilled at. You have a minute to set up your space and prepare for your scene.

Ready? Let's begin.

Magicians at work for approximately one minute. Note: With younger children, it may be more appropriate to have them all working individually within the whole group.

Teacher:

Just hold what you are doing for a moment and listen.

7. Generating ideas for Fioran

Grouping:	**As in Activity 6**
Strategies:	**Narration; discussion**
Administration:	**None**
Focus:	**To consider the advice that the magicians will give**

Teacher narrates:

As the magicians worked long into the night, they talked (or thought) about what advice they could offer to the princess. What could they say to someone who was faced with such a problem? Fioran had promised to marry the knight, whom she knew to be a kind and loving man. Yet, he had just told her his secret: that when the moon rose high and full in the sky, he was drawn to the forest, where he turned into a werewolf.

Now, magicians know about how to deal with these sorts of difficulties; they have spells, they have potions, they have a lot of good common sense and a great deal of experience.

Teacher:

Let's come out of role for a moment.

In your groups (or with a partner) take some time to consider the kinds of advice the magicians of the court would offer.

Remember, Fioran is the daughter of the king. Whatever advice you give may be taken and acted upon. There may be consequences—for Fioran, for Feolf, and for you, the magicians!

You will need to be ready to give your advice to the princess when she comes to speak to you.

Teacher circulates and listens as students, in their groups (or with a partner), talk about the advice they would give.

8. Fioran seeks advice   5 minutes

Grouping:	**As in Activity 7**
Strategy:	**Teacher in role as Fioran**
Administration:	**Perhaps a large piece of "royal" fabric to represent Fioran; tambourine**
Focus:	**To consider the advice they will give**

Teacher:

In a moment, Fioran will be coming to hear what advice you have for her. It will be important for us all to hear everyone's advice.

Here's how we can do it.

Let's arrange our groups (or pairs) around the room so that, as Fioran moves through the magicians' quarters, we will all see and hear their conversation. [Groups (or pairs) place themselves in a circle.]

Sit down so that you can see the magicians and hear the advice they give to Fioran.

Let's decide which group Fioran will visit first. [They do]

In order to help our story, you will continue with your magician's work.

You will know when I am at your door because you will hear me knocking. That will be your signal to stand ready to meet Fioran in your roles as magicians.

Are we ready to begin? Will the first group stand and begin your work?

Teacher (perhaps wearing the "royal fabric") approaches the first group and taps on the tambourine three times. Each time the teacher approaches a different group, she or he will want to say something a little different. Some examples:

Teacher in role as Fioran:

- Magicians, I am at a loss. I so dearly love Feolf and he loves me. We are to be married tomorrow and yet I hesitate. What help can you give me?
- Magicians, I know that this is a problem that you have not encountered before but I am desperate for your help. I would appreciate any advice that you can offer that will help me to decide what I should do.

- Good sirs and ladies, your advice is always so wise. I am just a young woman who knows little about the world outside my father's castle. What should I do?
- I have heard many excellent suggestions already but I know that your colleagues regard the work you do as superior. What do you think I should do?
- Although you are the last I visit tonight, I value your advice no less. As my father's magicians, you know me well and love me as your own. How can you help me decide what to do?

Serious treatment is the key to this strategy. Teacher listens hard to everything that is offered and all ideas are welcomed and treated seriously. For example, if one group suggests killing Feolf:

Teacher in role: How could I have him killed? He is so kind. He has never hurt anyone. Surely, even as a wolf, he still has his noble heart?

You do not have to judge the advice nor do you have to make a decision based upon it. The purpose here is to have the students wrestle with the problem.

Teacher: Out of role for a moment. Before we go on, you might like to talk to each other about what you have just heard. [Groups talk together]

9. What actually happened   *2 minutes*

Grouping:	**Whole group**
Strategy:	**Reading aloud (teacher)**
Administration:	**The storybook**
Focus:	**To hear what the magician in the story told Fioran**

Teacher: You gave some splendid advice to Fioran. It was not an easy task for you and you all handled it with great imagination and skill.

Let's hear how our author, Jenny Wagner, continues the story:

Teacher reads from: *The magician who would have liked to marry her himself* to . . . *and there was still no sign of him.*

10. Waiting for the wedding   *3 minutes*

Grouping:	**Whole group**
Strategies:	**Narration; improvisation; teacher in role as court official**
Administration:	**None**
Focus:	**To explore dramatic irony. In the real world, we all know what has happened but in the fictional world of the drama, we must act as if we do *not* know.**

Teacher: Think for a moment of yourself as one of the wedding guests and find a place somewhere in the room. [They do]

What might you be wearing? What sort of journey have you had? What are your expectations for this day?

Teacher pauses to let students think as wedding guests.

<u>Teacher narrates:</u>	All the guests, dressed in their finery and anticipating a royal wedding, found themselves waiting long past the appointed hour.
	That hour grew into hours. The wedding guests were hungry and cold. These royal halls were not well heated and there was little room around the great fire. What had happened? Why the delay?
<u>Teacher:</u>	Let's see those guests as they wait and talk together.
	What sorts of things would they say to each other?
	Look around the room; see someone from another court whom you haven't seen since the last great occasion. Make eye contact.
	In a moment, you will move *slowly* through the crowd toward one another. You may find that there are more than two of you; just be sure that everyone has someone to speak with.
	Are you ready? Let's begin.

Students should talk together just long enough to establish themselves as guests—about a minute.

<u>Teacher in role as a court official:</u>	Ladies and gentlemen: His Royal Highness, the king, has asked me to say that he thanks you for your patience but that we must be realistic. It does not seem as if the groom will appear. The king has consulted with his court magician and the magician has suggested that *Perhaps [Feolf] went for a walk in the forest. If so, I doubt we will see him again. There are too many wolves in that forest.*
	The king expresses his appreciation of your presence but suggests that you all make preparations for your return journeys.

After a brief pause (during which there may be some sort of "buzz" of reaction):

11. Sadness descends   2 minutes

Grouping:	**Whole group**
Strategy:	**Reading aloud (teacher)**
Administration:	**Story text as adapted below, inserted into the storybook**
Focus:	**To deepen the feeling content**
<u>Teacher:</u>	Just sit down where you are and listen to what happened next.
<u>Teacher reads:</u>	*The king decreed a time of mourning. There was to be no more music and no more feasting: they would eat nothing but turnips and fish cooked in ashes. The minstrels hung their lutes on the wall, and a deep silence settled on the castle.*
	Fioran shut herself in her room and wept for days and days. No one could comfort her, not the ladies of the court; not even the court magician, who kept sending her little presents; and not even her father, the king.

12. What are they thinking? 5 minutes

Grouping:	**Individuals**
Strategy:	**Writing in role**
Administration:	**Paper and pencils**
Focus:	**To express the thoughts of the protagonists**

Teacher:

Come and get a piece of paper and a pencil and find a place by yourself.

There are three people in the castle whom we know would have very strong feelings about what has happened: the king, the magician, and Princess Fioran. Which one of these people would you want to find out more about?

Choose one only.

Are you the king whose daughter has been left? Are you the magician whose advice the princess took? Are you the princess? What is she thinking?

Think quietly in the role you have chosen, about the kinds of thoughts that would be going on inside your head during this time of court mourning. Imagine how you must feel about the situation. What is going on in your mind as you experience the loss of Feolf? There must be all sorts of things to think about.

Begin writing what's in your mind as you take on the role you have chosen. [They do]

Students should write for at least three to four minutes—longer if there is time. Often students will stop writing but go on thinking, then find they have something to add.

Teacher:

I'd like you to finish what you are writing now.

Read over what you have written and underline the sentence or phrase that best expresses what is in your mind at this time.

13. Hearing the thoughts of others 3 minutes

Grouping:	**Individuals**
Strategy:	**Tapping in**
Administration:	**Students' writing from previous activity**
Focus:	**To get a sense of perspective by hearing the thoughts of others**

Teacher:

Read over the words you have underlined and commit them to memory.

Students will need a minute for this.

Teacher:

Close your eyes.

When you feel my hand on your shoulder, just say those words aloud.

After you have spoken, drop your head so that I will know you have finished what you want to say.

Listen to the thoughts of the others as they break through the *deep silence that has settled on the castle.*

Teacher moves around the class, putting a hand on each student's shoulder until all have spoken. Leave a silence.

14. Building the questions for Feolf   5 minutes

Grouping:	**Whole group**
Strategy:	**Brainstorming**
Administration:	**None**
Focus:	**To discover Feolf's life as a werewolf**

Teacher: We've just heard those powerful thoughts of the people in the castle. But what of Feolf? What was happening to him all this time? What must his life be like now that he must remain transformed?

What kinds of questions would we want to ask him?

It may be enough to solicit a few questions as examples or you may want to formalize the question-asking as illustrated in the following Option.

Option

14a. Building the questions for Feolf   5 minutes

Grouping:	**Whole group**
Strategy:	**Brainstorming**
Administration:	**Chalkboard and chalk or chart paper and felt pen**
Focus:	**To develop questioning skills**

Teacher: What might be some of the questions that would give us a good sense of what has been happening to Feolf and what it is like for him to be a werewolf all this time?

The questions that we ask are going to be important, so we must think about them carefully.

The questions that the students devise remain on the board for reference and prompts during the interview that follows. Building these questions also allows the teacher to have ideas about what is going to be asked although she or he needs to be prepared for others that may arise.

15. Meeting the werewolf   5 minutes

Grouping:	**Whole group**
Strategy:	**Hot seating**
Administration:	**Chair; a piece of fur to symbolize Feolf**
Focus:	**To hear Feolf's story**

Teacher: Would you be willing to accept me as Feolf?

> This piece of fur will be a reminder that we are talking to Feolf the werewolf who is, in his heart, still a knight. Who will ask the first question? *[Establish who will ask the first question before going into role]*

Teacher: Are we ready to meet Feolf?

Teacher sits on the chair and drapes fur piece across shoulder. There is no need to try to look like a wolf. What is important is that you take on the attitudes and points of view that Feolf would have as a wolf. Perhaps a certain wariness?

Teacher in role as Feolf: I haven't spoken to human beings for a very long time. Thank you for your interest in me. I know you must be wondering what these months have been like for me.

Stop talking and wait for the first question.

*During the hot seating, teacher integrates the information from the text as it appears from **Autumn came, and Feolf stayed in the forest** to . . . **and only the crows in the fir trees heard him and flapped their wings.***

Your objectives are to let students know how Feolf is surviving and what his hopes are. Don't be surprised if you are asked, "How did you become a werewolf?" Your guess is as good as ours!

Some suggestions:

- As a result of a spell?
- It's simply a part of your family's history.
- You don't know. There have always been werewolves; it is part of your nature.
- It only happens to second sons.

Whatever you say, it is serious and thoughtful and noble. You need to avoid the "hairy palms" scenario, though it may come up. If it does, you simply say, "There are many foolish tales. Look at my paws, there is no hair there."

Note: The more you talk, the less they will question. Keep your answers short to encourage language development.

When you feel that the questions are beginning to wane and that you have provided enough information for them to understand what has happened to Feolf,

Teacher in role as Feolf: Talking in what is now my second tongue is very tiring. I must seek food and then I must rest. Winter is not an easy time for animals. Thank you for hearing my story.

Teacher gets up, leaving the chair and moving to a neutral space.

16. The end of the story

16. The end of the story *As needed*

Grouping:	**Whole group**
Strategy:	**Reading aloud (teacher)**
Administration:	**The storybook**
Focus:	**To complete the story**

<u>Teacher:</u>   Are we ready to hear how Feolf almost loses his life? [They are]

<u>Teacher reads from:</u>   *The king's sorrow deepened with the coming of winter* to the end of the story.

At this time teacher shows class the last picture in the book.

<u>Teacher:</u>   It does not say if Fioran changed into a wolf, but what do you notice in this picture? What conclusions could you draw?

Students will begin to discuss the implications of this picture and hypothesize about the future life of this couple. Here is where some of the key questions may come into play.

---

17. Reflection *5 minutes*

Grouping:	**Whole group**
Strategy:	**Discussion**
Administration:	**Key questions on a note card (optional)**
Focus:	**To make application of some of the key concepts**

<u>Teacher:</u>   Turn to the person next to you for a moment and talk about what you have just heard.

When students have had a moment or two to chat, continue.

<u>Teacher:</u>   I wonder how different the story would have been if Feolf had not told the princess Fioran his secret?

What ideas do you have?

Think back to our ideas about werewolves. What's now changed?

What other examples can we think of where we've judged people without really knowing them?

When we ask people for advice, what do we need to keep in mind before acting on that advice?

Turn to the person next to you and talk about your experiences in the drama today. You might want to share which parts you remember most vividly.

What do you think it was that made you remember them?

What other stories have you heard like this one?

After a few moments of pair sharing,

<u>Teacher:</u>   What ideas would you like to share with us?

Of Dark and Wolfish Things **83**

Let the discussion develop.

There are a number of other reflective strategies that you may want to use. Some suggestions:

- writing the story of Feolf and Fioran ten years later
- retelling the story as a storyboard
- planning a royal wedding; the menu, the invitations, designing the wedding outfits, or the wedding presents (this could include researching the period for foods and costumes)
- learning some music of the period and/or a court dance
- writing "The ballad of Feolf and Fioran"

Resources

Cusworth, R., and J. Simons. 1997. *Beyond the Script*. Sydney, NSW: Primary English Teaching Association of Australia.

Wagner, J., and R. Roennfeldt. 1995. *The Werewolf Knight*. Sydney, NSW: Random House.

Materials

Activity 1:   Overhead projector; overhead of wedding guests at court (left page)

Option 1a: Table; large piece of "royal" fabric; piece of fur; sheet of parchment or a copy of a page of illustrated manuscript; small dagger or long sword; goblet; cloak; candle stick with a burnt-down candle; quill pen

Activity 2:   Chart paper and felt pen

Activity 4:   Tambourine

Activity 5:   The storybook

Activity 8:   Piece of "royal" fabric; tambourine

Activity 9:   The storybook

Activity 11:   The storybook

Activity 12:   Paper and pencils

Activity 14a: Chalkboard; chalk or chart paper; felt pens

Activity 15:   Chair; piece of fake fur

Activity 16:   The storybook

Activity 17:   Key questions on a note card for prompts (optional)

CHAPTER EIGHT

All Dried Up and Blown Away

Based on *The Dust Bowl*
written by David Booth and illustrated by Karen Reczuch

Why Did We Choose This Story?

■ *The Dust Bowl* by David Booth offers an engaging story of a particular family and enables participants to consider the universal themes inherent in it.

■ The illustrations offer evocative insights into the characters lives, thoughts, and feelings. Karen Reczuch, the illustrator, captures the temperature of the times both literally and figuratively—you can almost taste the grit in your mouth!

■ The story is beautifully written as a series of memories told through the voice of the grandfather. The lives of this all-male household are rich with love and caring—for the past, for each other, for the land—and with hope for the future. There are ample opportunities for a wide variety of language arts activities.

■ A study of the prairies both in Canada and the United States is a part of the curriculum. The place of the prairies in North American history is central to the growth of both nations. The story provides a narrative-history framework for study as an alternative to the more analytical and distanced perspectives of most textbooks.

■ *The Dust Bowl* serves as a lens through which we can examine a number of curriculum areas: the Great Depression, its effects on migrant labor, child labor, and the evolution of social policies (social studies); climatic changes that cause a land to "dry up and blow away" (environmental studies, geography); qualities that enable families to survive hardship and how these qualities have contributed to our nation building.

■ An examination of families under duress is part of the hidden curriculum that not only helps students to understand the importance of community but, subtextually, the importance of community to themselves as students.

■ The young protagonist has the same sorts of worries and concerns shared by all children who sense that there is something happening that even adults are unable to control.

■ Many students have some connection with the land, either presently or in the past; many have parents and grandparents who farmed and whose stories they know.

■ We live in a world that is constantly being disturbed by natural calamities. The awsome power of nature's destructive forces is engaging to students and adults alike.

Key Understandings and Questions

■ What is it that people need to sustain a sense of family when facing situations that are beyond their control?

■ What would or could make you leave your family home?

■ What sorts of qualities would you need to have in a time of natural disaster?

1. *Imagining the land and the homestead*   *2–3 minutes*

Grouping:	**Whole group**
Strategy:	**Discussion**
Administration:	**Overhead projector; overhead of back-cover picture**
Focus:	**To engage the students in the context**

Teacher turns on overhead projector to reveal back-cover picture of the land.

<u>Teacher:</u>	Imagine the people who lived on the prairies some sixty years ago. They may in fact be just like our grandparents or great-grandparents.
	It was a good place to live and people had all that they needed.
	I wonder what connections you might have with this picture? [Students share ideas]

2. Drawing the homestead and the land   6–10 *minutes*

Grouping:	**Groups of 5–6**
Strategies:	**Drawing; discussion**
Administration:	**Chart paper; colored pastels; charcoal; masking tape**
Focus:	**To build belief in role**

Teacher:

Get into groups of five or six. Each group has pastels and charcoal and a large piece of paper.

At a time when the land to be worked was so vast, and the towns so far apart, people had to be pretty self-dependent, not just for making a living but for everything else—animals, their food, clothing, housing and entertainment—when they had the time.

I wonder what your piece of land looked like? Remember that there were no such things as Safeway, no Wal-Marts, no 7-Elevens, no recreation centers, no TV.

Together, your task is to draw what your farm looked like. As you draw together, make your group into a family.

How would your drawing show that you had everything you needed? What would you need to have in order to be self-sufficient?

Each member of your family has many responsibilities; talk about these as you draw a picture of your land and the homestead.

When the drawings are almost completed, you will need to warn your students to finish up.

Teacher:

Just another minute to complete your picture.

When the drawings are complete, have groups hang them up. Be sure that everyone has a chance to see all the "farms." Depending upon time and objectives, you may want to talk about the drawings.

Teacher:

Because sharing was a large part of the community life, and there were few stores and those stores were often very far away, what would you, as a family, be able to offer your neighbor?

OR

If you do not want to discuss the pictures, their presence on the walls serves as a backdrop for the drama.

Teacher:

These pictures show how each farm family lives and the different duties that each member of the family has. Thank you. We will need these to remind us of the good times.

3. The family on the farm

Grouping:	**As for Activity 2**
Strategy:	**Tableau**
Administration:	**Space for each group to work independently; caption strips; felt pens**
Focus:	**To discover the responsibilities of farming life**

Teacher: Find your own space and using everyone in the group, create a tableau with your bodies of the family at work on the farm. Don't forget to include the children. Each one of them will be responsible for one or more jobs.

As groups are working toward completion, teacher gives each group a caption strip.

Teacher: If you were to see this picture in your family photo album, what caption would be under the photograph that would show the goodness of the land and of your lives? For example: "In the barn at harvest time."

Each group has a caption strip. Write the caption down in large-enough print so that we can read it as we see your tableau.

When the tableaux are ready, decide together the order of the tableaux.

Teacher: Gather around this first group.

Close your eyes. When the tableau is formed and still, I will say, "Open," and you will see the tableau as I read the caption.

No talking; just look carefully.

The groups move from tableau to tableau, hearing the caption and "reading" the tableau.

Teacher: Return to your original spaces and talk together about what you have seen and heard.

After a minute or two,

Teacher : What sorts of things did you talk about that would be important for all of us to hear? [They share]

OR

Teacher may wish to extend the strategy through tapping in. In this case, the strategy is used at the time each tableau is seen, or after all tableaux have been observed without comment. Then go around again, this time using the tapping in strategy as suggested.

3a. Discovering the inner life 10 minutes

Grouping:	**As for Activity 2**
Strategy:	**Tapping in**
Administration:	**None**
Focus:	**To express thoughts in role**

<u>Teacher:</u>	Just hold your tableau. I am going to come around and when you feel my hand on your shoulder, just speak as the person in the tableau, the thought that is in your mind.

Teacher may invite students observing to contribute to the questions. They may want to tap in themselves or they may prefer you to tap in, using their questions.

Be sure to leave your hand on the student's shoulder for the time he or she is speaking. Don't rush this. Sometimes a student won't speak. Just wait until you are sure that nothing is coming and then move on without comment.

You do not need to ask every member of the tableau to speak. Remind students that they only need to say a few words. Thus, the lifting of your hand is also a signal that they can stop speaking.

Some examples of the kinds of questions that get at the focus:

- What is your responsibility? (*to get at task*)
- What time do you get up in the morning? (*to build belief*)
- How do things change with the season? (*to build time*)
- Apart from work, what sort of things do you do together as a family? (*to build belief*)
- What are the rewards of this kind of life for you? (*to build personal commitment*)

<u>Teacher:</u>	Thank you. We are beginning to get an idea of the world these people inhabit. We'll now move on to the next group and see what they will add to our understanding.

Teacher continues until all groups have been seen and heard.

<u>Teacher:</u>	(*To whole group*) Before we move into the story, what have we seen or heard that helps us to understand better how the people in our story live their lives?
	Let's listen now to the story to find out more about what farming was like for people in those days.

4. Building the background 2 minutes

Grouping:	**Whole group**
Strategy:	**Reading aloud (teacher)**
Administration:	**The storybook**
Focus:	**To add information**

<u>Teacher reads from:</u>	*When your grandma and I . . .* to *. . . how fast things change on a farm.*

5. Meeting the protagonist/s *3 minutes*

Grouping:	**Whole group**
Strategy:	**Building questions**
Administration:	**Overhead projector; overhead of the man and the woman on the steps; chalkboard or chart paper and black felt pen**
Focus:	**To let the picture raise the questions we need to ask**

Teacher: Now, we know that sometimes things will happen in our lives that will change us forever.

Teacher shows the overhead picture of the man and the woman on the steps.

Look at this picture. Don't talk about it, but think about these people and what might be happening in their lives.

I wonder what questions we need to ask?

Before we list them, talk to your partner and see what sorts of things we might want to find out about. [They discuss for about one to two minutes]

Depending on the experience of the class, the next activity may not be necessary. If it is, Teacher writes five or six questions suggested by the class on the board.

Teacher: We are creating this drama and, as we ask our questions, we will be hearing new information that might trigger new questions. The questions on the board are just to get us started.

6. Developing the narrative *10 minutes*

Grouping:	**Whole group**
Strategy:	**Sculpting or molding**
Administration:	**A chair without arms; a large hankerchief to wipe the sweat away; copy of letter in pocket**
Focus:	**To build empathy**

Teacher: Would you be willing to allow me to become the man in the picture? [They agree] I will need your help.

Teacher sits on the chair in a neutral position.

Teacher: Would you be willing to mold me as this man?

Teacher may choose to use the suggested prop to help the students see the role. Note: You should not become the person in the picture until the students create you.

Teacher: You will need to look as carefully as an artist does in order to be able to help me represent the feelings and thinking of this man. When you are satisfied that I am "right," you may begin to ask your questions.

The students, one by one, come and shape the teacher.

You will find there may be a great deal of discussion before students agree on the representation and the changes that they need to make in order to achieve that. You may ask while they are shaping you such questions as:

- Does this look right? Have I got it?
- What do you need to change on me to help you believe that I have become the person in the picture?

When the students are satisfied, teacher relaxes position.

Teacher:	In a moment, I will go back into role and be ready for your questions. But before I do, how will we address this person?
	What is his name? [They decide]
	Who will ask the first question?

If students aren't used to facilitating themselves, you may want to ask the students if they would like to appoint someone to call on volunteers.

Teacher again assumes the man's position.

Teacher:	Just let me check that I have got it right? [Students adjust if necessary]
Teacher in role as the man:	Hot night! You want to ask me some questions?

7. Foreshadowing 3–4 minutes

Grouping:	**Whole group**
Strategy:	**Hot seating**
Administration:	**As above; storybook with letter from the bank inside (be sure this is easy to get to quickly)**
Focus:	**To provide information about what has changed**

Teacher's job in role is to provide students with the kind of information that will prepare them for what is to come. For example,

- I'm worried about the crops this year. ***By June the heat had burned them down to nothing.***
- It hasn't rained for over two weeks. What rain there is can't soak into the hard ground. The well is not in very good shape.
- ***Too hot to work in the day, too hot to sleep at night.***
- I've borrowed money, as we always do to buy seed. We've harvested what we could, but I owe a lot to the bank.

Remember, it is not your job to tell them the story but to give them the information they ask for and to set in the implications of that information. When working as teacher in role, the less you have to say, the more the students are pressed into speech.

After about three to four minutes,

Teacher:	Nice talking to you folks. Think we'd all better try and get some sleep, if we can.

Teacher leaves the chair.

8. The heart of the story   *5 minutes*

Grouping:	**Whole group**
Strategy:	**Narration**
Administration:	**The storybook**
Focus:	**To confirm what is being lost**

<u>Teacher narrates:</u> And the man stayed outside for a long time in the close, hot darkness, thinking about all that he had been through over the years to put down roots and build a place for a family.

Teacher picks up storybook and continues reading from,

> **Then the rain stopped completely** to . . . *for some, farming was becoming a slow way to starve.*

Omit next paragraph and continue on next page from,

> **I'm not saying we** . . . to . . . *those insects could stop a train.*

9. The letter from the bank or "Man in a Mess"   *3 minutes*

Grouping:	**Whole group**
Strategy:	**Teacher in role as man; silent follow-along reading (students)**
Administration:	**Letter from the bank (Figure 8.1) for each child, one for the teacher; letters in envelopes addressed to fictitious names (e.g. Mr. Vant, RR3, Rosehill, SK)**
Focus:	**To put the students into the dilemma of the story**

<u>Teacher:</u> Find a space by yourself.

Sit down and think about what has happened to the man you have just met.

I am going to put an envelope down beside each of you. You will know when to pick it up and open it.

Teacher hands out envelopes, returns to the chair, sits down, and reassumes the role. While taking the letter from the envelope,

<u>Teacher in role:</u> I wonder how many of my neighbors have received this letter and if they will be reading it at the same time as I am.

Teacher opens the letter slowly and begins to read it aloud. The idea here is that the students will pick up your signal, open their letters, and read along silently with you.

10. *The dilemma*

Grouping:	**As for Activity 2**
Strategy:	**Discussion**
Administration:	**None**
Focus:	**To understand the implications of the choices they are having to make**

Teacher:

Gather in your family groups near the drawing of your farm.

Talk about what options you have in the face of the events that have occurred over these last few years.

Will you go on? How could you manage to stay? If you leave, where will you go?

Will you all be able to stay together? [Students talk]

11. *Meeting at the community hall*

Grouping:	**Whole group**
Strategies:	**Narration; discussion; teacher and students in role**
Administration:	**None**
Focus:	**To determine what is being lost; what is important to hold on to**

Teacher narrates:

The people knew that they were not alone in hearing from the bank and that it was important that they meet with their neighbors to talk about what was happening in their lives and to their community, and of their plans for the future.

Teacher:

How can we create a sense of a community hall in our classroom? It's important that what we create, we can all agree on and believe in. [Students make suggestions and effect them]

Just come in your family groups and sit down.

Note: The community meeting is held with the students facing in the direction opposite to the one in which they were working with the teacher in role. This technique helps the students to identify the different drama events spatially and is useful to them in reflection.

Teacher joins the meeting in role as one of the crowd.

Teacher:

Well, folks, I don't know what to do. We've talked it over at my place and we're pretty much at a loss. I thought that maybe someone here might have some suggestions.

What have you been talking about?

What are you thinking of doing?

The discussion that follows is an opportunity for people to say how they feel about their lives in the community, on the farms, after all the years they have invested in the land. Keep this informal. You are as helpless as they are and your job is to listen, to validate, to question the easy decisions. For example:

- It's so sad. We've been here all our lives, some of us.
- How can you afford to go east?
- What will you do with your parents? Will they be strong enough to go with you?

Try not to rush; allow time for the students to explore all their options.

Teacher in role: Well, folks, it's late. It's clear things can't go on as they are. We'll have to sleep on it. Good night.

12. What does this mean for our family?   *1 minute*

Grouping:	**Whole group**
Strategy:	**Narration**
Administration:	**None**
Focus:	**To synthesize the meeting and prepare for the next strategy**

Teacher narrates: The people left the meeting quietly. There was not much they could say. So many ideas were in their heads and so much despair.

For some, who had never wanted the responsibilities demanded by the land—even for them the thought of having to leave at this time, not by their own choice, was upsetting.

They knew that they would have to make a decision and that that decision would affect the rest of their lives.

That night, they couldn't sleep. They took out their diaries and began to write about this terrible decision they were having to make.

13. What are we to do?   *5 minutes*

Grouping:	**Individuals**
Strategy:	**Writing in role**
Administration:	**Letter from the bank; pencils**
Focus:	**To concretize their thinking and feeling**

Teacher: Find your own private space and using the back of the letter from the bank, write about the decision you have to make. It may not be the final decision. Rather, you are writing about your thoughts and feelings as you think about the decision you have to make. [They write for three to four minutes]

Underline the sentence that expresses most clearly what is in your mind at this time. Commit it to memory.

It is the thinking and feeling that goes into the making of this decision that we need to hear. [They choose a line]

Teacher does not go on until he or she is sure that everyone has completed the task.

Teacher: Fold up your letter and put it somewhere on your person.

This technique is a useful one for it is a way of symbolically reminding the students of what they have been thinking.

14. Collective thinking of the community   *3 minutes*

Grouping:	**Whole group**
Strategies:	**Voice collage; reading aloud**
Administration:	**Student writing; the storybook**
Focus:	**To create a collective experience to situate the end of the story**

Teacher: When I put my hand on your shoulder, say your line aloud so that we can all hear it.

Once you have spoken your line, put your head down and listen to your neighbors' thoughts and feelings. [Students speak aloud the sentence they have underlined]

Putting their heads down is a management technique to remind you of which students have spoken.

Teacher reads from: *The winter was the last straw for many farmers* to the end of the story.

15. Making the story part of our own experience   *5 or more minutes*

Grouping:	**As for Activity 2**
Strategy:	**Reflection**
Administration:	**None, or you may wish to use the farm drawings from Activity 3**
Focus:	**To connect the particular (the story) to the universal experience**

Teacher: Go back to your family groups (and gather round your picture of the farm) and talk together. What is it about a farm that keeps people there?

After a few minutes,

Teacher: Let's gather together as a group and share some of your ideas.

What does this story tell us about the people who still live on farms today? What about the people who live in other places where nature rules their existence? What keeps them there?

What sorts of qualities would you need to have in a time when it seems that your lives "have just dried up and blown away" as it did for so many in the time of the dust bowl?

Think about today, when it seems that our lives are drowning in natural disasters like floods, or being blown apart by tornadoes, fire, earthquakes, or frozen by ice storms. I wonder how (or if) it is different from then?

If appropriate:

Teacher: How did your study about this period help you in the drama? How was learning through drama different from other learning experiences?

Resources

Andrews, J. 1990. *The Auction.* Illustrated by K. Reczuch. Toronto, ON:
Douglas & McIntyre.

Booth, D. 1996. *The Dust Bowl.* Illustrated by K. Reczuch. Toronto, ON:
Kids Can Press Ltd.

Hess, K. 1999. *Out of the Dust.* New York: Scholastic.

Materials

A copy of the story, with stickies to mark the parts to be read aloud

Activity 1:   Overhead projector; overhead of the back cover picture
or any picture that shows the vastness of the prairies

Activity 2:   Plain chart paper and pastels (multiple colors) and charcoal; masking tape

*Note: The softer drawing materials are in keeping with the mood of the illus-
trations, but you could also use crayons. Use felt pens only as a last resort, as
they resonate a different energy.*

Activity 3:   Felt pens and caption strips

Activity 5:   Overhead of the man and woman on the porch; chalkboard and chalk or chart paper and a black felt pen

Activity 6:   Chair without arms; handkerchief (optional)

Activity 9:   Letters from the bank (as many as there are students)
and one for the teacher (see Figure 8.1), all in addressed
envelopes

Activity 13:   Pencils

Township Bank of Saskatchewan
24 Main Street
Saskatoon, Saskatchewan

November 27, 1931

Dear Sir:

We are sorry to have to inform you that the Township Bank can no longer lend your family any additional money. We understand that your situation is not through any fault of your own but rather one of the results of the hardships of nature.

Nevertheless, our board is very clear that it will take no further financial risks. We are sorry for any additional burden that may result from this decision.

Please arrange an appointment with us as soon as possible to discuss the repayment of your present loan.

Sincerely,

Robert H. Smith

R. H. Smith
Manager
Township Bank

FIGURE 8.1   Letter from Bank

May be photocopied for classroom use. © 2004 *Into the Story through Drama* by Carole Miller and Juliana Saxton. Heinemann: Portsmouth, NH.

CHAPTER NINE

A *Wealth of Knowing to Be Reaped*

Based on *Josepha: A Prairie Boy's Story*
written by Jim McGugan and illustrated by Murray Kimber

Why Did We Choose This Story?

■ Our reasons for choosing this book begin with the language that McGugan uses in the telling of this story. His first-person narrator is a younger child who is befriended by Josepha.

■ Without losing the child narrator's tone of admiration for the older role model, McGugan is able to capture in the most subtle of ways the language of an adolescent immigrant who is proficient enough "to earn a one-dollar wage" but not enough to advance out of the primary row of a one room school.

■ "Fitting in" is something that we all understand. Those students who feel that they do not fit in, for whatever reasons, will find resonances in this story with their own lives and experiences.

■ Those of us who teach will recognize the teacher's sense of helplessness as she watches a student with "a wealth of knowing to be reaped" leave the classroom for the attractions (and necessity) of a job that pays.

■ The world of school a century ago is not all that different from the world of school today, and immigrant children still experience the realities of building a life in a new country. *Josepha*, a story set one hundred years ago, can be used to provoke reflection on present conditions of education and discussion of the kinds of human qualities that lie beyond knowledge and skills.

Key Questions and Understandings

- What is the relationship between a good education and a good human being?
- In what ways does school influence our future?
- The relationship between the teacher and the student has an importance beyond the curriculum.

---

1. Setting the context   *7 minutes*

Grouping:	**Whole group in pairs, one volunteer to be the first Master**
Strategy:	**Game**
Administration:	**Chairs**
Focus:	**To create a metaphor through which we can consider education, then and now**

Teacher: Before we begin our drama, we are going to warm up with a game called Masters and Movers. This is a very challenging game because it demands keen observation and the ability to read subtle signs.

This is a very difficult game and, like all games, playing by the rules is the key to its success. The rules however, require that the students listen carefully.

Note: If the class has an even number of students, then the teacher will play. Or one student may volunteer to become the "warden," whose job is to make sure that the rules are being followed.

Teacher: First, I would like a volunteer to bring a chair to begin the circle of chairs. Please stand behind your chair. You are a B and all Bs are "Masters."

The rest of you are to find a partner. Decide who is A and who is B and together bring one chair to continue building the circle.

As, sit on your chair. Bs, stand behind your partner with your arms behind your backs.

Bs, you are the Masters. As, you are the Movers.

Now, we have an inner circle of Movers seated on chairs and an outer circle of Masters standing behind the chairs with their arms behind their backs. Only one chair, the first chair to be brought to the circle, has no Mover.

It is the job of that chair's Master to find someone to fill the chair.

Master, you will do this simply by winking at any Mover in the circle.

When eye contact has been established, the Mover must then move as quickly as possible to sit in the empty chair.

However, if the Master senses that his or her Mover is about to move to fill the empty chair, that Master can stop the Mover by placing his or her hands firmly on the Mover's shoulders.

Masters, you need to keep a careful watch so that you don't find yourself with an empty chair.

When a move has been successfully completed, there will be a new empty chair and a new Master looking for someone to fill it.

The goal of the game for the Master is always to keep someone in his or her chair.

Signaling can only be made by eye contact. There will be no talking.

Master of the empty chair, your goal is to get someone to sit on your chair.

Other Masters, your task is to keep someone in your chair at all times. Movers, there is always a better Master somewhere else. You are always looking to move. Your task is to make your moves as quickly and subtly as you can. Let's try a couple of rounds to sort out the problems. [They do]

After the game has been played so that everyone has had a chance to move, As and Bs exchange places and the game resumes. After most players have had a turn,

Teacher: Right, let's stop there. Just talk to your partner about what was going on in your mind when you were a Master and when you were a Mover.

After a minute of pairs' discussion,

Teacher: What were some of the things that were going on in your minds in this game? [They share as a whole group]

I wonder what situations in our lives have held us back from doing something that we wanted to do, or were invited to do? [They share]

The story that we are going to explore today happened about a hundred years ago. The game we have just played, although not one that children played in those days, is a metaphor—another way of looking at what happens in the story.

2. Creating the meeting room   **4 minutes**

Grouping:	**Whole group**
Strategy:	**Designing**
Administration:	**Chairs; tables (optional); chalkboard or something to write on**
Focus:	**To create a meeting room in which we can all believe**

Teacher: The first thing that we have to do is to turn our classroom into a meeting room, one that will include a place for someone who will run the meeting and who can be seen by everyone. Also, we will need to have a chalkboard or something to write on that can be seen by all. Now, how will we begin?

This is a very informal activity as students move furniture and discuss its arrangement. Of course, if you are already in a classroom setup with desks, this activity may not be necessary. On the other hand, working together to create a "fictional space" is a useful activity for helping students to build their roles in the drama.

| Teacher : | Good. Now I'm going to ask you to find a chair and stand behind it. I would like you to do this in alphabetical order of last names, starting with the first chair there. [*Teacher indicates*] |

There may be a bit of negotiation during this activity as students sort out the correct alphabetical order when there is more than one name beginning with a certain letter. You may want to do a roll call so that everyone has a chance to check for accuracy.

3. Meeting with the administrator of the school district   *5 minutes*

Grouping:	**Whole group**
Strategies:	**Mantle of the expert; teacher in role**
Administration:	**Foss County School District folders, containing the name tags and Formal Assessment of Progress forms (Figures 9.1 to 9.3), 1 for each student; jacket, glasses, or old leather briefcase**
Focus:	**To introduce the problem; to provide a sense of expertise and background**

Teacher:	Now we are ready to begin our drama. I am going to walk away and when I come back, I will be someone different. As I speak, you will discover who I am and who you are in the drama.
	Remember, if you are having a problem for whatever reason, you may put up your hand and say, "May we go out of role for a moment?" and we'll stop and sort things out.
	Any questions? Are we ready?

Teacher walks away from the playing space. He or she puts on a pair of glasses or a jacket or picks up a briefcase to indicate a role change. Remember, there is no need for you to do anything other than to adopt the attitude and points of view of a school district administrator in 1900.

Teacher turns and walks briskly to the chair at the head of the meeting room.

| Teacher in role: | Good day, ladies and gentlemen. Dr. James, the district inspector for the Foss County Board of Education, sends his regrets and looks forward to meeting you individually in your schools at a later date. My name is Miss (or Mr.) _____ (*use your own name*) and Dr. James has appointed me to represent him. Please, do sit down. This meeting will be very informal. [Everyone sits] |

The role of Dr. James's representative is used so that if someone asks a question or voices a concern that you do not feel you want to handle, you can always say, "I'll certainly refer that to Dr. James and I know he will be happy to address your concerns when he can."

| Teacher in role: | It is my pleasure to welcome you into our prairie community and to meet you all in person. It seems that we have been corresponding for such a long time but, of course, it takes a long time to process your teaching credentials. |
| | We know we have selected the most highly qualified students from the Teachers Academy. You have been chosen to work here in Foss County |

School District because of your resourcefulness, your strength of character, and the demonstrated excellence of your teaching abilities. These are the qualities upon which you will be drawing as you take on teaching in our isolated rural communities.

To help us get started, I will give everyone a folder. In it you will find a name tag. I ask you to remember that now that you are qualified schoolteachers, you are to be addressed by your title and last name only.

Therefore, Miss or Mr. will precede your last name on the name tag. The district wishes you to understand that first names are not to be used in the interests of maintaining respect for your positions.

When you have completed this task, please pin the name tag so that it can be seen by everyone.

As students complete the task, you might want to check with them that they understand what's going on. You can do this by saying, "Out of role for a moment." You might also want to remind them that, as excellent teachers, they will have exceptional handwriting and/or printing skills.

Once name tags are in place,

4. The schoolhouse   5 minutes

Grouping:	**Whole group**
Strategy:	**Discussion**
Administration:	**Pictures of prairie schoolhouses, soddies (sod covered huts), and life on the prairies (available in libraries)**
Focus:	**To provide information about the differences between school today and school long ago**
Teacher in role:	Dr. James felt that it would be helpful if we met as a group, since all of you will be dealing with similar school populations and common issues. We have been able to use some of the new technology to obtain photographs that will help you to come to a deeper understanding of the challenges you will be facing.

Teacher hands out pictures while speaking.

Teacher in role:	As you receive these photos, please discuss with the person sitting beside you how the information in these pictures may affect your teaching. When you are ready, we will share our thoughts, concerns, and your questions. Of course, Dr. James would be the best person to talk to, if only he could be here.
Teacher:	I'm going to go out of role now.
	In a moment, we are going to talk about these pictures. Should we speak in role or out of role?
	Whatever we choose to do, we will use what we know about schools today to help us see the sorts of challenges that the inspector's assistant spoke of. Remember that we are looking for the challenges that

we will face as new teachers one hundred years ago. [They make a choice]

If students choose to talk out of role, give them a minute or so before saying, "Right, back in role, now." If students prefer to talk in role, give them about three minutes, reminding them that they are looking for the challenges for them as teachers.

| Teacher in role: | I would be so interested to hear some of the challenges you see ahead for you. |
| | Please remember that although you will be very far away from the district office, we do hope to see each of you at least once a year. You always have our support. |

However the students choose to summarize their observations is acceptable.

5. The case study   6 minutes

Grouping:	**Whole group**
Strategies:	**Mantle of the expert; reading aloud (teacher)**
Administration:	**Foss County School District folders; the storybook**
Focus:	**To introduce the protagonist as a model for the challenges that these young teachers will face**

Teacher in role:	Now, to an important issue.
	As you have observed, life on the prairies can be very hard and the inspector of education is concerned about the number of children who leave school early, often with less than a grade-four education. He feels that too many of our students, particularly those from immigrant families, are leaving school before they have become familiar with the English language or with the culture of our nation. I am sure that you have met some of these children already in your teaching practice.
	The inspector is proposing that we retain our students until at least the age of fourteen or until they complete grade six. The inspector is looking to you new, fresh young teachers to initiate his proposal.
	My purpose today is to provide you with practice in diagnosing and assessing some of the issues that may arise for you in attempting to follow the inspector's request.
	The case we are presenting is drawn from our files of a few years ago but, it is representative of the kind of child you will be meeting.
	In your folders you will find a Formal Assessment of Progress Report on which to record your observations after you have been introduced to the case.
Teacher reads from:	The beginning of the story to *He did not know how.*
Teacher in role:	Please take a few moments to record on your assessment forms what you know or can infer about this student.

Now, what do we know about this student? What further questions arise? What else do we need to know in order to help this individual be a better student? [They respond]

Teacher in role fields the answers, folding them, where appropriate, into new questions. The focus here is to pull information from the students, not to feed it in.

6. Hard work equals a good wage   8 *minutes*

Grouping:	**Whole group**
Strategy:	**Reading aloud (teacher)**
Administration:	**The storybook; Formal Assessment of Progress Report**
Focus:	**To move from the general situation to the lens of a particular student, Josepha**

<u>Teacher in role:</u> Let me continue with this case study. Perhaps your questions will be answered.

<u>Teacher reads from:</u> *Later Josepha wept. Miss sat by him* to *Farmers made farmers*

<u>Teacher in role:</u> Now that we have a better picture of this child, what else do we know about him? What do you think are his areas of strength and where do you think his challenges lie? Please record your observations. [They do so for one or two minutes]

Before we discuss these new questions and observations, I have our district visual art inspector's rendition of Josepha's situation. It may provide added information.

7. Exploring Josepha's thoughts   7 *minutes*

Grouping:	**Whole group**
Strategies:	**Voice collage; tapping in**
Administration:	**Overhead projector and overhead of the picture of Josepha sitting in the primary row or one copy of the picture for each pair of students**
Focus:	**To explore the thoughts and feelings of Josepha**

Teacher turns on overhead projector with the picture of Josepha (or hands out copies of the illustration of Josepha) sitting in the primary row.

<u>Teacher in role:</u> While we can never really know what is in a child's mind as teachers, we need to understand what a child such as Josepha might be thinking and feeling as he sits in the primary row day after day. Take a moment to consider his perspective. If Josepha could speak his thoughts in English, what might we hear? Close your eyes and hear his thoughts.

When you feel my hand on your shoulder, just say those words aloud. Remember to use your teacher voice so that we can all hear. Who will be the first to begin?

Teacher moves around the room, gently touching individual students on the shoulder. Note: It is helpful to the students if you leave your hand on their shoulders as they speak.

After all students have spoken, teacher acknowledges their contributions.

Teacher in role: What new insights have you gained? What do we know or what can we infer about Josepha's learning or home situation?

As new teachers soon to be in similar situations, what do you think are the key issues in this case study?

Again, teacher in role fields the responses and facilitates the conversation. Students will be drawing on their own classroom experience, as well as that given in the story.

8. Interviewing Josepha   *6 minutes*

Grouping:	**Pairs**
Strategies:	**Interviewing; private instruction**
Administration:	**Pairs of chairs, set randomly around the room; paper and pencil**
Focus:	**To practice interviewing an older child who is going to leave school**

Teacher: Out of role, everyone.

I'd like you to find a partner, someone with whom you have not been working today. You and your partner take your chairs to your own space. Make sure that you will not be disturbing anyone else. [Students do this]

Decide who is A and who is B. [They do]

As, you will be the teacher.

Bs, you will be Josepha. While I meet with the As, think about your situation at home and at school and where you need to be now.

As, may I see you here for a moment?

Teacher gathers students away from the Bs, and checks that everyone is an A.

Teacher gives the following private instruction to As:

Teacher: As a new schoolteacher, you know that the inspector will look very favorably on you if you can keep all your pupils in school for the whole year. Your task is to try to persuade Josepha to stay. If he cannot, then persuade him to come back after the harvest. What sorts of ideas do you have that might help to keep him in school? You know your task. Think hard about it while you return to sit on your chair and I talk to the Bs. [As return to their chairs]

May I see all the Bs over here, please? [Bs gather]

Teacher gives the following private instruction to Bs.

Teacher: As Josepha, you probably have a number of reasons for leaving school. What might some of those be? Quietly, we don't want the As to over-hear. [Students offer]

Your task is to listen very carefully to what Miss (or Sir) says. Is there anything that she (or he) can offer you that might persuade you to stay or to think about coming back to school at some time? I would like you to be thinking about your reasons for leaving as you go and stand behind your chair.

(*To everyone*) Right. You each know your task and it looks as if we are ready to begin. Josepha, you will begin the improvisation by saying, "Are you ready to see me, Miss (or Sir)?" When you are ready, begin.

As students improvise for two or three minutes, teacher circulates to listen in and pick up on what is being said. It is useful to have paper and pencil ready to jot down anything you hear that may be helpful to you in the next strategy.

9. Hearing from both sides   10 *minutes*

Grouping:	**Two groups (teachers and Josephas)**
Strategies:	**Circle within a circle; students in role; teacher in fringe role**
Administration:	**Chairs in two circles, one around the other**
Focus:	**To hear what was said and how it was received**

<u>Teacher:</u>

Stop there.

Would the teachers please bring their chairs into a circle in the middle of the room?

Josephas, please bring your chairs into a circle around the chairs in the middle. Be sure that your chair is close enough to hear what the teachers say, but not to interfere. Just listen to what the teachers say, but do not comment or talk to one another. Your task is to hear what is being said and to think about how it reflects what you have just experienced.

Are we ready?

<u>Teacher in fringe role:</u>

Well, I am wondering how your meeting went. This matter of keeping children in school is not so easy to do, gathering from some of the things I heard being said.

What concerns do you have?

The teacher's job is to facilitate the conversation. You want to hear from as many students as possible, so keep the talk mediated through you and focused on the challenges of keeping children in school. You may want to use the following probes:

- I'm sure your task would be easier if you did not have to deal with the language problems.
- It must be very difficult to discover which children have an aptitude for schooling and which children are simply not ready for it.
- Remember, our job is to keep children like Josepha in school.
- What kind of a future do you see for this child?

These probes can reveal useful information that otherwise might not be given.

A Wealth of Knowing to Be Reaped   **107**

After teacher and students have talked together for about five minutes,

<u>Teacher in fringe role:</u>	Thank you very much for your reflections. I can see that there are many concerns that need to be addressed if children are to be encouraged to stay in school.
<u>Teacher:</u>	I'd like to talk to the Josepha's now. Please change places. [They do]
<u>Teacher in fringe role:</u>	I understand that your teacher is anxious for you to stay on in school. I wonder if he or she really understands why you cannot or do not wish to stay. What sorts of things would make it possible for you to stay?

Again, your task is to let the conversation develop, keeping it on track and in role. You may want to interject with the following probes:

- What sort of responsibility do you feel toward your parents?
- How important is it, do you think, for your sisters to have an education?
- Surely your older brother can carry the load? After all, it's not a very big holding that your father has.
- When you look into your future, what do you see for yourself?

After about four or five minutes,

<u>Teacher in fringe role:</u>	Thank you very much. I can see that for someone so young, there are a great many concerns and responsibilities. School must not seem to be as important for you.
<u>Teacher:</u>	Perhaps it would be a good idea just to go back to your partner and talk out of role about the improvisation and what you have just heard in the circles.

After a few minutes,

<u>Teacher:</u>	Who has anything that they would like to share?

There will generally be a fair amount of conversation after this extended strategy and it is interesting for everyone then to do a whole-group reflection. Students may want to talk about the in-role work or they may want to reflect on the strategy itself. It is useful to talk about both, leaving the "how we did it" until the "what happened inside" is explored.

10. The end of the story   6 minutes

Grouping:	**Whole group**
Strategy:	**Reading aloud (teacher)**
Administration:	**The storybook**
Focus:	**To discover what Josepha decides to do**
<u>Teacher:</u>	Let's hear what happens in the story of Josepha. As you listen, remember how you were thinking and feeling when you were in role, talking to your teacher.
<u>Teacher reads from:</u>	*Josepha studied his teacher's eyes* to the end of the story.

11. A letter to Josepha

Grouping:	**Individuals**
Strategy:	**Writing in role**
Administration:	**Foss County School District folders, containing sheet of paper and pencil**
Focus:	**To think as Josepha's teacher; to synthesize**

Teacher:

I'm going to ask you now to begin thinking as Josepha's teacher. You know what has happened and how you feel about it.

As you are thinking, just move quietly to your folders.

Take the pencil and extra piece of paper and find your own space in the room. Sit down quietly and begin writing a letter to Josepha.

You may begin by saying thank you for the present he gave you. What is more important, however, is to let him know how you feel about what has happened and your hopes for his future.

Leave a good five minutes for this activity. Don't worry if students stop writing. You can say quietly, "I can see that some people are doing some deep thinking about what they are writing." When most students have filled a good part of the page,

Teacher:

Just stop there. Reread what you have written.

When you have read through, go back and underline the phrase or sentence that you feel best sums up what you wanted to say to Josepha.

Commit that phrase or sentence to your memory.

12. Saying goodbye

Grouping:	**Whole group**
Strategy:	**Conscience alley**
Administration:	**An old pair of boots**
Focus:	**To hear each other's words; to find catharsis**

Teacher:

May I have someone volunteer to take on the responsibility of becoming Josepha? You don't have to speak but you must listen very hard to what is being said as you move slowly down the line. [Student volunteers]

The rest of you will make two lines, leaving enough room for Josepha to walk between them. [They do]

As Josepha moves slowly between you, say to him the sentence or phrase that you have memorized.

Be aware that only one person should speak at a time so that Josepha can hear what you have to say.

Any questions?

Sometimes students are a little confused, especially if they have not worked with this strategy before. Clear up the difficulties before you begin, so that the power of the feelings is not interrupted.

| Teacher: | Perhaps it would help us to make it more real if Josepha was carrying the boots he has just been given. What do you think? |

If they agree, teacher gives the boots to the volunteer. Generally, students see the importance of the boots as a significant prop.

| Teacher: | Are there any questions before we begin? Remember, Josepha, walk slowly enough so that you hear every thought. |

If there are any problems as the strategy moves along, just stop it quietly and sort it out and then ask the student in role as Josepha to start again. After the walk is over,

| Teacher: | Thank you. Just find someone to talk to and share your thoughts together. |

13. *Reflecting and connecting*   *5–10 minutes*

Grouping:	**Whole group**
Strategy:	**Reflection**
Administration:	**None**
Focus:	**To make a connection between then and now**

| Teacher: | Let's just gather here and talk about what has happened. [They do] |
| | If we could see into the future, what sort of future do you think there would be for someone like Josepha? |

Other possible questions:

I wonder how this story connects with our own lives or the life of someone we may know?

What might be the connections between the game that we played at the beginning of our drama and Josepha's story?

Schools are very different today but I am wondering what parallels you can see?

It seems to me that Josepha was a good person. I wonder if his schooling would make him an even better person?

OR

They say that a good education is the making of a man or woman. Without that education, what sorts of regrets might Josepha have?

Suggested Extensions

- Bring the drama to the present day: create a tableau that best illustrates the issues faced by those students for whom school represents difficulties, challenges, or marginalization, and then caption it.
- Interview parents or grandparents or caregivers for a story about when they went to school.

OR

- Interview parents, grandparents, or caregivers about what they think is different about school today from when they were at school.

Resources

You will need to have a pioneer picture resource set for activity 4. These are available in a library.

Adams, J., and B. Thomas. 1985. *Floating Schools & Frozen Inkwells: The One-Room Schools of British Columbia*. Madeira Park, BC: Harbour Publishing.

Bedard, M. 1997. *The Divide*. Toronto, ON: Tundra Books.

Beeler, C. F. 1991. *The Girl in the Well*. Calgary, AB: Red Deer Press.

Bouchard, D. 1997. *Prairie Born*. Paintings by Peter Shostack. Victoria, BC: Orca Books.

Harvey, B. 1990. *My Prairie Christmas*. New York: Holiday House.

———. 1986. *My Prairie Year*. New York: Holiday House.

Kalman, B. 1999. *Homes of the West*. St. Catharines, ON: Crabtree.

———. 1999. *Who Settled the West*. St. Catharines, ON: Crabtree.

McGugan, J. 1995. *Josepha: a prairie boy's story*. Calgary, AB: Red Deer College Press.

Morck, I. 1999. *Five Pennies: A Prairie Boy's Story*. Calgary, AB: Fifth House.

Patent, D. 1996. *Prairies*. New York: Holiday House.

Reynolds, M. 1999. *The Prairie Fire*. Victoria, BC: Orca Books.

———. 1997. *The New Land: A First Year on the Prairie*. Victoria, BC: Orca Books.

Storey, V. 2003. *Learning to Teach: Teacher Preparation in Victoria, BC: 1903–1963*. Victoria, BC: The Bradley Project, Faculty of Education, Univeristy of Victoria.

Turner, A. 1985. *Dakota Dugout*. New York: MacMillan Publishing Company.

Materials

Activity 1:   Chairs for each student; one for the teacher

Activity 2:   Chairs; tables perhaps (optional); chalkboard or something to write on

Activity 3:   Foss County School District folders, containing name tags and Formal Assessment of Progress forms, one for each student; jacket, glasses, or old leather briefcase

Activity 4:   Pictures of prairie schoolhouses, soddies, and life on the prairies

Activity 5:   Foss County School District folders; the storybook

Activity 6:   The storybook; Formal Assessment of Progress reports

Activity 7:   Overhead projector; overhead of the picture of Josepha sitting in the primary row (p. 5 of the story); or copies of the picture (one for each pair)

Activity 8:   Pairs of chairs, set randomly around the room

Activity 9:   Chairs in two circles, one around the other

Activity 10: The storybook

Activity 11: Foss County School District folders, containing lined sheet of paper and pencils

Activity 12: An old pair of boots

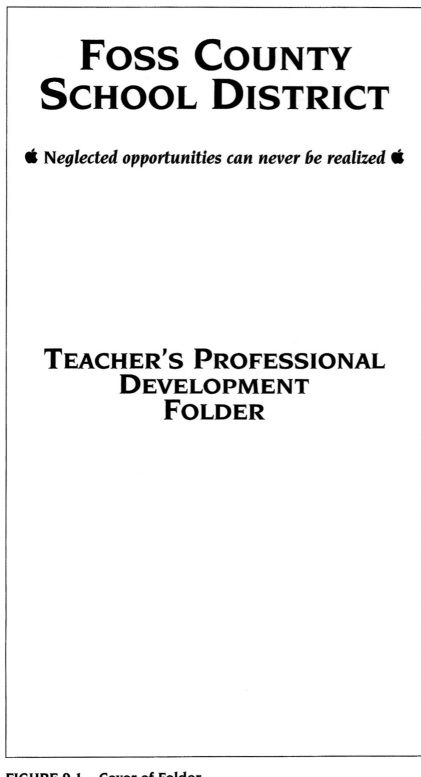

FIGURE 9.1 Cover of Folder

Foss County School District   Foss County School District

Foss County School District   Foss County School District

Foss County School District   Foss County School District

Foss County School District   Foss County School District

Foss County School District   Foss County School District

FIGURE 9.2   Name Tag Sheet

Foss County School District
Formal Assessment of Progress

Pupil _____   Age _____

Teacher _____   Date _____

Neglected opportunities can never be realized

FIGURE 9.3   Sample of Formal Assessment of Progress Form

CHAPTER TEN

An Understanding Heart

Based on *Only Opal: The Diary of a Young Girl*
written by Opal Whiteley and illustrated by Barbara Cooney

Excerpts selected by Jane Boulton

Why Did We Choose This Story?

■ We were drawn to the story because of the opportunity to work with a rich historical primary source and because the story is told from the child's perspective.

■ "Opal has the gift of expression to a high degree which enabled her to reveal, through her diary, something of that inner world of childhood whose doors so rarely open to outsiders" (Bradburne 1962, 68).

■ Barbara Cooney, the illustrator, has an extraordinary gift for capturing the essence of the text and for understanding perspective—not only from what is written but also in terms of what we need to see.

■ Students will identify with Opal's narrative and with the importance that imagination plays in all our lives. The changes in Opal's life, although particular to her, will be easily recognized by many children. Her story and the language she uses to tell it provide a sense of distance that invites students to explore personal feelings in a safe way.

■ There are an infinite number of curricular connections that may be accessed through the source. Parallels to a number of fairy tales are evident. The ways in which the author gives her animals and things in nature human characteristics and personalities serve as rich models for students' imaginative writing.

■ The historical frame opens up opportunities for research, particularly for personal stories from grandparents and great-grandparents.

■ Opal Whiteley, born around 1900, was an early naturalist. "She saw with the eye and mind of a scientist and the heart of a poet," notes Bradburne (1962, 46) and her understanding of nature foreshadows environmental issues.

■ Other curriculum areas to explore: forestry and logging, single-resource towns, the significance of childhood in a nation's psyche, the development of child labor laws, government agencies for children's welfare. All of these topics offer potential for curriculum integration.

Note

"The papa," Mr. Whiteley, although not mentioned in this text, was a part of Opal's life and does appear in her diary. Therefore, we have taken the liberty of including him. We have made some minor adjustments to the text and omitted portions of the text in order to facilitate the drama. All changes are included within the structure.

Key Understandings and Questions

■ The writings and perspectives of children are rarely acknowledged as valid reading for adult audiences.
■ The imaginary world plays a significant role in helping children cope with extraordinary circumstances.
■ Beyond food, clothing, and shelter, what makes life worthwhile?

1. Building context   5 minutes

Grouping:	**Groups of 5**
Strategy:	**Puzzles**
Administration:	**1 cut-up (as a puzzle) photo of Opal (see Figure 10.1) as a young woman for each group (in envelopes)**
Focus:	**To create the metaphor for Opal's life; thinking as an author**

Teacher: Groups of five, please.

In your group of five, assemble the pieces of the puzzle that you find in the envelope. You have five minutes.

When you are finished, look carefully at the picture in front of you. Together, decide what words you would use to make this face come alive in a novel.

When students have all completed the puzzles and begun the conversation,

Teacher: Who would be willing to contribute to our knowledge of this woman? [Students share]

Teacher: Drama is about putting the pieces of a puzzle together in order for us to build a common understanding. We may see differently because we all come from different life experiences. It is those experiences that we bring to the drama and, in sharing them, the way we build common understandings.

Now leave your picture intact for a moment.

2. Meeting Opal

Grouping:	**Whole class**
Strategies:	**Reading a picture; discussion**
Administration:	**Overhead projector; overhead (without text) of the first picture (little girl sitting on rocker)**
Focus:	**To explore the picture for information and context**

Teacher:
I'd like you to look very carefully at the first picture from our story. The name of the child in this picture is Opal. An opal is a gemstone and when you look into it, it is full of all sorts of different colors.

Teacher turns on the overhead, letting a moment or two pass while the students look at the picture.

Teacher:
Look carefully at this picture. What do you see? [They describe]

As the students are talking, you might want to question them as to how they can validate their impressions. For example, Student: She looks lonely. Teacher: Where do you see that? This enables students to move from the general to a more sophisticated reading of the picture.

Teacher:
When might this picture have been taken?

Students are drawing on their knowledge of historical time.

Teacher:
What assumptions can we make about Opal's life from this picture? What is your sense of her life? [Open discussion]

We are beginning to put the pieces of this child's life together. This is the puzzle we will be exploring—the life of a child that is reflected in the face of the woman whose picture you have just been solving. Her name is Opal Whiteley and this is her story.

Please collect the pieces of the puzzle and put them into the envelope. I'll be around to collect them.

Teacher collects envelopes.

3. Discovering Opal's life

Grouping:	**Whole group**
Strategy:	**Observation; discussion**
Administration:	**2 Overheads (if available); the double-page picture on the next two pages can be overlapped on 1 projector**
Focus:	**To open the subtext of Opal's life**

Teacher:
Now that we have so many ideas about the first picture and met Opal, let's look at two others to see what they tell us about her life in a small logging community in Oregon. Talk to the person next to you about what you see. [They do]

From what we have just seen and talked about, what can we say about the world in which Opal lives?

There are many things that students may comment on. For example, the first picture was really taken outside the house. If such an observation is made, teacher might ask, "Why might the photographer not be invited inside? What does that tell us?"

When the students remark on the woman in the doorway,

Teacher: Yes, look at her stance, the way she is standing. What do you imagine she might be saying to Opal? [They suggest]

Some examples: "Hurry up!" "The fire is almost out." "Supper's waiting!" "Don't forget to wipe your feet." "Feed the dog."

Teacher: Good, you are all thinking like authors. You'll need your imaginations as we enter the story.

4. Opal and "the mama"   10 *minutes*

Grouping: **Pairs**
Strategy: **Improvisation**
Administration: **As in Activity 3**
Focus: **To explore a relationship**

Teacher: Make a pair with the person next to you.

As authors, you are going to create the dialogue between Opal and the woman in the doorway.

I wonder who would be speaking first? [They decide as a whole group]

What might she be saying? [They offer]

What might be Opal's response? [They offer]

With your partner, decide who will be Opal and who will be the woman.

Decide on your two lines of dialogue. [They do]

Now you have your role and your lines. Just where you are, give those lines a try. [They do]

Now, switch roles. Same lines. [They do]

Just talk about that with your partner. Now create and add two more lines so that your dialogue reflects what you see and "hear" in the picture. [They do]

Let's reflect the picture in terms of this space. Move away from each other so that you find the right distance between you. [They move]

There will be lots of people speaking at once. You will really need to focus on one another and block out everyone else. It will help if the woman uses Opal's name. You may want to try using her name at the beginning, in the middle, or at the end. Let's try it. [They do]

Let's hear some of these dialogues. We'll listen to hear the different kinds of relationships that the words between these two people give us.

Teacher hears some or all, depending upon the willingness of the class.

| Teacher: | Just talk for a moment with your partner about some of the assumptions we could make about the relationship between Opal and the woman. |
| | Those dialogues will help us to understand Opal's life. |

5. Introducing the story   *5 minutes*

Grouping:	**Whole group**
Strategy:	**Reading aloud (teacher)**
Administration:	**The text as rearranged below; first picture (portrait of Opal) on overhead**
Focus:	**To paint a picture with words in a different way; to make us aware of Opal's role in the family**

Teacher introduces the book by showing the cover and reading the title.

Teacher:	*Only Opal: The Diary of a Young Girl.* The book is illustrated by Barbara Cooney. You may have read other stories that she has illustrated. The story we are using for our drama is true. It was written by Opal Whiteley one hundred years ago. This story, like her name, is very unusual.
	Opal Whiteley was about five when she began her diary. What is even more special is that there is very, very little literature—stories or diaries—written by children that anyone thought worth publishing, especially so long ago when children were to be "seen and not heard." I'll tell you the story of how Opal's diary came to be published at the end of our drama.
	Listen to Opal's words as you look again at her picture.

Picture appears on overhead.

Teacher reads:	*My mother and father are gone.*
	The man did say they went to Heaven
	and do live with God,
	but it is lonesome without them.
Teacher:	Think back to that second picture where we saw Opal with the wood. As you hear her words, see how you can become your own illustrator by creating the pictures of Opal's story in your own mind.
Teacher reads:	*The mama and the papa where I live say I am a nuisance.*
	I think it is something grownups
	don't like to have around.
	The mama sends me out to bring wood in.
	Some days there is cream to be shaked into butter.
	Some days I sweep the floor.
	The mama has like to have her house
	nice and clean.

| Teacher: | In her diary, Opal refers always to *"the* mama" and *"the* papa." I wonder why? |

Teacher leaves this question hanging.

Teacher:	*...I did not go to school today*
	For this was wash day
	And the mama needed me at home.
	The mama says that is my work,
	But it takes a long time—
	And all the time it is taking I have longings to go explores.
	...When I feel sad inside
	I talk things over with my tree
	I call him Michael Raphael
	It is such a comfort
	To nestle up to Michael Raphael
	He is a grand tree.
	He has an understanding soul.
Teacher:	So why "the mama" and "the papa"? [Students offer possibilities]

Some examples: "a foster child"; "an adopted child"; "Maybe that's the way they talked in those days."

6. Creating Opal   10 *minutes*

Grouping:	**Whole group**
Strategy:	**Role on the wall**
Administration:	**A life-size craft paper cutout of a child; felt pens of various colors; masking tape**
Focus:	**To synthesize our perceptions of Opal through the use of adjectives**
Teacher:	What words might we use to describe Opal? What adjectives could we use?
	Can we write them here on this piece of paper—on the outline of Opal—so that we have a record to help us with our drama?

Teacher places a large piece of paper, cut in the life-size form of a child approximately four feet tall, on the floor.

| Teacher: | When you have a word or phrase that describes Opal, come and write it somewhere on this outline. [They do] |
| | Let's hear the kind of person we think she is. |

As the teacher reads (or students read), the teacher has an opportunity to comment that people are often made up of contradictory qualities (if there are contradictions) and to note those qualities that give Opal strength and a sense of herself.

Teacher:	Children orphaned a hundred years ago needed to be strong both inside themselves and physically.
	As I hang up this outline as a reminder for our story, think about the couple who adopted Opal.

7. Creating the community   7 minutes

Grouping:	**Whole group**
Strategies:	**Thinking in role; tableau; mime**
Administration:	**Chair for each student**
Focus:	**To imagine the people in the community**

Teacher:	In the next part of our drama, we will be imagining that we are those people who lived in the logging community where Opal was orphaned.

Take time with the following role-building ideas and questions. Students need that time to consider and engage with the background for the roles they will be undertaking.

Teacher:	Some of you may have known her birth parents, some of you might have only heard about their deaths. All of you know the hardships of life in this logging community.
	You know how difficult it is to raise a family in such circumstances: men away cutting trees, often for days at a time, always with the presence of danger from falling trees, the weather, the sharp tools. It was a life of great responsibility.
	The women with their responsibilities, often alone, having to fend for themselves and take care of community concerns—and always the children to be fed, housed, clothed, and schooled. You have heard that there is an important meeting tonight to do with one of the children.
	Think in your own mind as if you were a member of this community. What brought you here? How long have you lived here? Are you alone or do you have family? How many children? What kind of work do you do? Remember, everyone worked in those days, in the home, in the forests, in the fields.
	Look across the room and find your place in this community. When you hear the next signal, begin to think as that person as you move to that place and find a position for your body that helps us to see what kind of work you do. Look around the room and see where you will be. You have ten seconds to go to that place and freeze. You will really need to focus on your thoughts. What's going on in your life? What might you be thinking about?
	As we count down from ten, you will move across the room to your place and freeze in that position. [They do]
	Use your peripheral vision to see your neighbors. [They look]
	When you hear the next signal, you will bring your work to life. As you work, one of the things you may be thinking about is the meeting that

has been called for tonight to discuss the future of a child in your community. Begin. [They mime for about twenty to thirty seconds]

Freeze. In a moment, still in role, you will take a chair and place it in this area ready for a meeting with the members of the community where Opal has been orphaned.

I am going to take on a role, too, and you will know who I am by what I say.

Are we ready to begin our meeting?

8. *The meeting in the schoolhouse*   10 *minutes*

Grouping:	**Whole group**
Strategy:	**Teacher in role as a respected member of the community; students in role as community members**
Administration:	**Chairs set out for meeting**
Focus:	**To discover how we understand parental obligation; to set the mood and provide the information**

Teacher in role:

Friends! Thank you so much for coming. If you would just bring in your chairs, we can start. [Students create the meeting place]

Teacher sits.

Teacher in role:

It's good to see so many of you back on your feet. I know it has been a long winter, a time of sickness. Some of you have lost members of your family. All of us have lost working time and that means money.

We've come through a lot but there are still problems that we must solve and the best way to do that is to do it together. For tonight, we'll focus on our immediate problem.

As all of you know, Opal Whiteley has been orphaned and she has no other family. We have been keeping her with us temporarily but unfortunately, we already have so many mouths to feed that we must find her another, more permanent, place to live.

Those of you who know her know that she is a very loving child with a wonderful imagination. Although she is only going on six, she has been reading and writing since the age of three. She is very good with animals. She is, of course, a bit of a dreamer.

The decision about Opal is important because, as you know, the inspector of child welfare will be needing assurances that Opal is placed in a good home in our community.

What are your thoughts? What should we do? Before we hear from individuals, maybe it would be better to talk to your neighbor first. [They talk]

This discussion is about advice, concerns, and the value of a child to a home. This is something students know a great deal about. The responsibility for the discussion rests with the students. Teacher in role becomes simply a member of the community who listens, reflects, and clarifies. Teacher's job is not to run the discussion but to facilitate and to step back from a "leading" role to that of listener; someone who knows no more than the rest but who, like them, has experiences to share. Generally, it takes four to five minutes to build commitment. At any rate, stop while the discussion is still lively.

Teacher in role:	It's getting late and there is much yet to do before bedtime. We know that there are a number of you who might be willing to take Opal in. I'm sure someone will step forward in the next few days. She is a strong little girl and quite able to take on work around the house.
	Thank you for coming on such short notice.

Teacher gets up and moves away from the playing area to indicate that the role is being dropped.

9. Moving the story forward   *1 minute*

Grouping:	**Whole group**
Strategy:	**Narration**
Administration:	**As in Activity 8**
Focus:	**To tell how Opal came to live with the mama and the papa**

Teacher moves back to the group.

Teacher narrates:	After a few days of consideration, a man and his wife stepped forward and agreed to take Opal. They had no children of their own—yet. The wife was happy to have the company and the extra help, as her husband was often away in the woods. They hoped to be able to move on soon to a mill town where the opportunities were better and where Opal and other children (when they arrived) could settle. Let's listen again to Opal's diary.

10. Learning about Opal's life   *2 minutes*

Grouping:	**Whole group**
Strategy:	**Reading aloud (teacher)**
Administration:	**The storybook**
Focus:	**To feed in information**

Teacher reads:	*This morning my crow Lars Porsena*
	did walk on the clean table cloth
	He was tracking crow tracks
	in jam all over it.
	The mama picked me up.
	And right away she did spank me
	for his doing it.
	I had to scrub little rubs
	a long time to get it clean.

. . . The calf is Elizabeth Barrett Browning.
I think she will be a lovely cow
There are lonesome feels in her mooings
when her mother is away.
I put my arm around her neck.
It is such a comfort to have a friend near
when lonesome feels do come.
I took off my sunbonnet and tied it on her
so the sun wouldn't bother her eyes.
When I came home the mama did spank me real hard
and told me to go and find my sunbonnet,
and not to come back until I did find it.
I wanted to talk to Michael Raphael.

My dear pig followed me to school today.
School was already took up.
I went in first.
The new teacher told me I was tardy again.
Peter Paul Rubens walked right in.
The grunts he gave were such nice ones.
He stood there saying:
"I have come to your school.
What class are you going to put me in?"
They were the same words
I did say on my first day of school.
I guess our teacher doesn't have
Understanding of pig talk.
She came at him in a hurry with a stick.

---

11. *Meeting the inspector*   *7 minutes*

Grouping:	**Whole group**
Strategies:	**Narration; hot seating**
Administration:	**Chair for the mama or the papa, large shawl or flannel shirt**
Focus:	**To show the family situation in its best light**
<u>Teacher narrates:</u>	Some months went by and although he had never been seen in town before, the inspector arrived to interview one of Opal's adoptive parents.
<u>Teacher:</u>	Would you allow me to become the mama (or the papa)?

Would you all be willing to take on the role of the inspector? Remember that in those days, a hundred years ago, there would be no women inspectors, that was a man's job. But in drama we can be anyone.

I wonder what kinds of questions the inspector might have? The inspector knows nothing about this family, only that they were highly recommended. His questions will help him to get a sense of how things are going. What kinds of things might he be interested in finding out?

Talk to the person next to you. Think about some of the questions the inspector might have. [They do for a minute or two]

Let's hear some of those questions. [They offer]

What might be the very first question the inspector would ask?

Field a few questions to stimulate thinking.

Teacher:

Who is willing to ask the first question? [*Choose a volunteer*]

I'll sit on this chair, shall I?

Teacher puts on shawl or shirt and sits.

Teacher in role:

Good morning, inspectors. I am happy to meet you and to talk with you about Opal.

I know that you are concerned about her welfare and I am more than prepared to answer any questions.

Wait expectantly for the first question.

Depending upon the questions asked, teacher feeds in the following information:

- All is going well.
- She is a lovely child.
- We are the ideal parents for her.
- She's not the kind of child who requires a great deal of discipline.
- She reads a lot.
- She has quite an imagination.
- There are few children nearby, but she has made friends of the crow, the mouse, the cow, the pig, and who knows what else! You should hear the names she gives them!
- She takes her time with things.
- All in all, we are very satisfied.

Teacher comes out of role by leaving the chair and taking off the shawl or shirt.

Teacher:

Well, that was quite an interview! Inspectors, what are your impressions of Opal's situation with this family? Talk briefly to the person next to you. [They do]

Option

The Inspector's Report

If the students do Option 11a, insert it here. If not, move on

Teacher narrates: We know how carefully the parent answered the inspector's questions so that the right impression would be given.

Now we have a chance to talk to Opal.

Option

11a. The inspector's report		as needed
Grouping:	**Whole group**	
Strategy:	**Writing in role**	
Administration:	**Paper and pencil**	
Focus:	**To concretize impressions of the interview**	

Teacher: From what you have heard from the mama, you are now prepared to write a report of Opal's home situation.

What might be included in this report? Remember, it will be read by your supervisor so be succinct—that is, only the main points need to be addressed.

The tension that is at work here is that, of course, they know the feelings of Opal and they are faced with having to deal only with the knowledge that they have been given by the parent. After students have finished, teacher collects the writing and says,

Teacher narrates: We know how carefully the parent answered the inspector's questions so that the right impression would be given. The report was sent off to the supervisor and Opal remained with the family.

Now we have a chance to talk to Opal.

12. Talking to Opal		10 minutes
Grouping:	**Whole group**	
Strategies:	**Narration; hot seating**	
Administration:	**Chairs**	
Focus:	**To hear Opal's perspective; to validate what students know and to elaborate on that knowledge**	

Teacher: I wonder how Opal would answer questions about her life with the mama and the papa?

Who would be prepared to take on the role of Opal? We are looking for three or four of you to take on this role to show us Opal's attitudes and ideas.

The wonderful thing about drama is that we can become anyone.

We've just all been inspectors, who in those days were always men. Now, anyone can be Opal and it's very useful to have different points of view.

Teacher sets up three or four chairs for the volunteers in front of the group.

Teacher:

(*To Opals*) Although there are a number of you in role as Opal, only one of you needs to respond to each question. You will need to listen carefully to each other's answers so that the story fits together in order to help us create our understanding of Opal's life.

Of course, there is much that has happened that we have not heard about. But knowing what you know about Opal's life already, you can move away from the text and become your own authors of Opal's life. You have our permission to be honest. Just be sure to maintain the integrity of the story. The pieces must fit together.

What might Opal say that would give us a different perspective from that of her parents?

The rest of us will question Opal as ourselves, not in role. What would we want to know from Opal about her life? [Students begin to question]

Teacher may become a questioner along with students in order to model questions and to pick up on Opal's responses to enlarge the range of possibilities. This strategy should take about three to four minutes. Stop when the focus begins to wane.

Teacher:

Thank you, Opals. You have certainly helped us to see things from another perspective.

(*To students*) From what you have just heard, I wonder if there is any new information we could add to our knowledge of Opal? [They may be happy to move on without further discussion]

---

13. Moving on   **3 minutes**

Grouping:	**Whole group**
Strategy:	**Narration; reading aloud (teacher)**
Administration:	**Paper and pencil for each student; storybook**
Focus:	**To take us to the end of the story**

Teacher:

Take a piece of paper and a pencil and find a place again where you can be by yourself.

Teacher narrates:

Before the year was out there were many changes in Opal's life. You remember how, whenever Opal felt "sad inside," she would *talk things over with [her] tree . . . Michael Raphael . . . because he has an understanding soul?*

But even Michael Raphael would change.

<u>Teacher reads:</u>	*. . . Today I did watch*
	and I did hear its moans
	as the saw went through it
	There was a queer feel in my throat
	and I couldn't stand up.
	The saw did stop.
	There was stillness.
	There was a queer, sad sound.
	The big tree did quiver.
	It did sway.
	It crashed to the earth.
	Oh, Michael Raphael!
<u>Teacher narrates:</u>	Other things changed as well. Opal had new responsibilities. The mama had a new baby daughter of her own and Opal's life would change again as that little girl grew up. The papa had found a new job in a different mill town.
	Here are Opal's words:
<u>Teacher reads:</u>	*I am sitting on the steps for the last time.*
	Tomorrow we will move to a mill town.
	. . . I am going far away,
	but Angel Mother and Angel Father
	will be with me.
	Guardian Angels always know
	where to find you.

14. *Saying goodbye*   *3 minutes*

Grouping:	**Individuals**
Strategy:	**Writing in role**
Administration:	**Paper and pencil for each student**
Focus:	**To create the final piece of the puzzle**
<u>Teacher:</u>	Imagine you are Opal or the mama or the papa. You are moving to a new life with all its hopes and dreams. You are leaving behind an old life filled with memories and experiences—some good and some not so good.
	As the mama, the papa, or as Opal, write down one sentence that says what is in your mind about this change.
	Will it be a memory? You might want to start with, "I remember when . . ." or "I shall never forget . . ."

If you are thinking about the future, you might want to start with something like, "I hope that . . ." or "When we get there, I will . . ."

Have students write for one to two minutes.

Teacher: Stop writing now.

In a moment, you will bring that writing with you as we move toward the end of our story.

15. Re-creating the last picture   5 minutes

Grouping:	**Whole group**
Strategy:	**Building an image**
Administration:	**4 chairs; the mama's shawl to represent the baby; flannel shirt for the papa; an old book for Opal**
Focus:	**To provide a frame for the final strategy**

Teacher places two chairs side by side in the middle of the room. As this is done,

Teacher: Can we agree that these two chairs will represent the front seat of the wagon that will take Opal and her family away? This is where the mama will sit with the new baby, and the papa will sit beside her to drive the horse.

Teacher takes two more chairs and sets them behind and facing backward.

Teacher: These two chairs will represent the back of the wagon where Opal will sit.

All of the family's belongings must fit between the two wagon benches. How far apart shall we place them?

Students negotiate the wagon space and talk about what to take and what to leave behind. Teacher may need to remind them that there is only so much room and only one horse to pull the wagon.

Teacher: Now that we have our wagon, who would be willing to represent the papa? [A student offers] Put on this shirt and take your place in the wagon.

Who would be willing to represent the mama? [A student offers] Take the mama's shawl and use it to represent the new baby. Would you please join the papa?

Is there someone who would be prepared to represent Opal? [A student offers] Take this book (your diary) with you as you take your place at the back of the wagon.

When all three students are in place,

Teacher: Freeze this moment.

This is the last picture of the story.

Grouping:	**Individuals, all standing but for the three in the wagon**
Strategies:	**Voice collage; tapping in**
Administration:	**Students' writing in role from Activity 14**
Focus:	**To reflect in role**

Teacher: I'd like the rest of you to please come and find your own personal space around the wagon, keeping in mind the dramatic space that surrounds this wagon. Your bodies will become the frame for this picture. [They do]

Recall those words that you have just written. Close your eyes. Imagine as Opal or the mama or the papa. This is the last time that any of you will see your old homestead.

When you feel my hand on your shoulder, just say or read those words out loud.

After you have spoken your thoughts, sit down on the floor and listen to other memories and hopes.

Teacher moves around the class, putting a hand on each student's shoulder, until all are sitting. Be sure to leave your hand in place until the student has completed his or her thought. When all are seated, leave a silence—a space for reflection.

Teacher: Thank you.

Teacher reads: *Over the years the family lived in nineteen different lumber camps, and during that time, Opal kept a diary which she hid in a hollow log in the woods. When Opal was twelve years old, her stepsister, in a fit of temper, unearthed the hiding place and tore the diary into a thousand fragments. Opal picked up the pitiful scraps and stored them in a secret box. There they lay undisturbed.*

When she was twenty, Opal met a book publisher who asked to see her diary. Opal spent nine months pasting together all the little scraps of paper. It was like doing a giant puzzle, matching up the red and green and blue words. The publisher liked her stories so much that he published them in a book that was called **The Journal of an Understanding Heart.**

Teacher: Now, knowing the future for Opal and her family, look one last time at the past.

Pause.

Teacher: Thank you.

Out of role, everyone. Opal and the mama and the papa, please join us.

Grouping:	**Groups of 4; whole group**
Strategy:	**Reflection**
Administration:	**None**
Focus:	**To debrief**

Teacher: We've been inside the story for a long time. Just turn to the person nearest you, then join another pair and talk together about your experiences in the drama. [They do for a minute or so]

The following are suggestions for stimulating discussion and reflection. Often the students need some prompts to deepen the connections and to internalize the experience.

Teacher: This event happened almost a century ago and hundreds of miles away. When we think about the picture of Opal as a young woman and the ideas we first generated as authors to describe her, I wonder now how we might shift our descriptions? How differently do we look at that picture, now that we know more?

Many of us, too, have experienced changes in our lives, whether we are children or adults. Some of those changes happen *to* us and are hard for us to understand sometimes. I'm thinking about some of the things that happened to Opal over which she had no control. What is it about people that makes it possible for them to cope with all these changes? What qualities do you need to be able to deal with these kinds of experiences?

You might draw students' attention to the role on the wall from Activity 6, and they may wish to add other adjectives.

Teacher: When you look into an opal it is full of all sorts of different colors. Let's think about Opal's name once again. What sorts of things come to mind now?

We have used many drama strategies to explore Opal's story. If you were going to tell your friend about one, which one would you choose?

This last question allows students to consider their understanding of how drama "works" and is an important element in their learning. Notice the "how it worked" question comes after questions that explore meanings.

Resources

Boulton, J. 1997. *Only Opal: The Diary of a Young Girl*. Illustrated by Barbara Cooney. New York: Putnam & Grosset Group. (Out of print; available in libraries)

————. 1995. *Opal: The Journal of an Understanding Heart*. New York: Random House Three Rivers Press.

————. 1976. *Opal*. Arranged and adapted by Jane Boulton. New York: Macmillan. Out of Print.

Bradburne, E. S., and O. Whiteley. 1962. *Opal Whiteley, The Unsolved Mystery, together with Opal Whiteley's diary, The Journal of an Understanding Heart*. London: Putnam.

Materials

Activity 1: One cut-up photo of Opal as a young woman for each group (in envelopes)

Activity 2: Overhead projector; overhead of the first picture (little girl sitting on rocker, no text)

Activity 3: Two overheads—or one with pictures overlapping the double-page picture on the next two pages

Activity 5: First picture (portrait of Opal) on overhead

Activity 6: A life-size paper cutout of a child; felt pens; masking tape

Activity 8: Enough chairs to be set out for a meeting

Activity 11: A chair for the mama or the papa; shawl or flannel shirt

Activity 12: Four chairs for Opals

Activity 13: Paper, pencils for each student

Activity 15: Four chairs; the mama's shawl to represent the baby; flannel shirt for the papa; an old book for Opal

Activity 16: Students' writing in role from Strategy 14

More About Opal

There are almost one hundred characters named in Opal's original diary. Some characters in the diary who appear in the text:

Felix Mendelssohn a pet mouse, named after the great nineteenth century German romantic composer

Brave Horatius the dog, named after the legendary Roman hero of the sixth century B.C. who defended a bridge over the Tiber against Lars Porsena

Lars Porsena the crow, named after an Etruscan ruler who sought to restore the exiled Tarquinius Superbus to the Roman throne but was deterred by the bravery of Horatius

Michael Angelo Sanzio Raphael a grand fir tree, named after the great Italian painter of the sixteenth century

Elizabeth Barret Browning a pet cow, named after the nineteenth century English poet, one of the first female poets to use her own name rather than a male pseudonym

Peter Paul Rubens a pet pig, named after the Flemish painter who was knighted by King Charles I in 1629

An Excerpt from the Original Diary

Today the grandpa dug potatoes in the field
I followed along after.
I picked them up and piled them in piles.
Some of them were very plump.
And all the time I was picking up potatoes
I did have conversations with them.
To some potatoes I did tell about
my hospital in the near woods
and all the little folk in it
and how much prayers and songs
and mentholatum helps them to have well feels.

To other potatoes I did talk about my friends—
how the crow, Lars Porsena,
does have a fondness for collecting things,
how Aphrodite, the mother pig, has a fondness
for chocolate creams,
how my dear pig, Peter Paul Rubens, wears a
little bell coming to my cathedral service.

Potatoes are very interesting folks.
I think they must see a lot
of what is going on in the earth.
They have so many eyes.
Too, I did have thinks
of all their growing days
there in the ground,
and all the things they did hear.

And after, I did count the eyes
that every potato did have,
and their numbers were in blessings.
I have thinks these potatoes growing here
did have knowings of star songs.
I have kept watch in the field at night
and I have seen the stars
look kindness down upon them.
And I have walked between the rows of potatoes
and I have watched
the star gleams on their leaves.

(Boulton 1984, 29–30)

CHAPTER ELEVEN

A *Powerful Thirst*

Based on *Letting Swift River Go*
written by Jane Yolen and illustrated by Barbara Cooney

Why Did We Choose This Story?

■ All of our students are undergoing change all the time. Predictable physical, mental, emotional, and moral changes occur naturally as a part of growing up. Other changes are those which are unanticipated: accidents, family breakdown, death, and so on. Still other changes are imposed: job loss or career shifts, government edicts, wars, and natural disasters.

■ We are living on the cusp of the new millennium; anxiety and anticipation are in the air. The familiar "19" has disappeared forever from our calendars and our checkbooks, yet the "last century" is still a vital, as well as an historical, reference for our lives.

■ A Powerful Thirst can be seen as a resource for the integration of curriculum. The writing and illustrations are a perfect marriage, direct and recognizable yet evocative and metaphoric, opening possibilities for any number of language and visual arts activities.

■ There are many opportunities for students to research their own particular locale to make a connection with history and to see themselves as agents of change.

■ In those curricular areas of science, the material becomes a window for investigating environmental issues on a local or global scale.

■ The story is told in the first person, from a child's point of view, and it deals with things that are not always fair. As Jane Yolen writes in her author's note before the story begins:

The drowning of the Swift River towns
to create the Quabbin [Reservoir] was not a unique event.
The same story—only with different names—
has occurred all over the world
wherever nearby large cities have had powerful thirsts.
Such reservoirs are trade-offs, which, like all trades,
are never easy, never perfectly fair.

Key Understandings and Questions

- To let something go does not mean to forget it.
- How are we affected by changes that are decided by others?
- How do we make peace with those changes in our lives?

1. Imagining the town   *5 minutes*

Grouping:	**Whole group**
Strategy:	**Reading a picture**
Administration:	**Overhead projector; overhead of first illustration**
Focus:	**To introduce participants to the context of the story**

Teacher turns on overhead to reveal illustration.

Teacher: What do you see in this picture?

We are looking for the students to identify the high hills, low hills, valley and river, and the town in the distance. They may see many other things too. Finish the observation with:

Teacher: Those hills and the river will be important in our story.

Listen to the first line of our story. **When I was six years old the world seemed a very safe place.**

Bring your attention back to the picture again. What is in this picture that makes it a "safe place"?

We are looking for students to focus their observations in terms of what they see as safe signs; for example, mother and child, bridge, the high hills protecting the town, the protections of the stone walls, the fence in the meadow to contain the animals, and so on.

Teacher: What does this tell us about the little town and the people who live there?

The teacher holds a brief discussion to build the general tone of the town as context for the detail work that will follow.

2. Drawing the town of Swift River *15 minutes*

Grouping:	**Whole group**
Strategies:	**Drawing; brainstorming; discussion; reading aloud (teacher)**
Administration:	**Long roll of paper, colored pastels, masking tape**
Focus:	**To build belief**

Teacher:	Imagine you are the people who lived in this low-lying valley, surrounded by hills in the town of Swift River about fifty years ago. It was a time of great prosperity, hope, and renewal.
	The Second World War had just ended. A sense of safety and peace was in everyone's hearts.
	Swift River is a town filled with hardworking folks whose parents and grandparents have lived there all their lives. It is a good place to live and people have all that they need.
	I wonder what this town would look like?
	Before you begin drawing the town, what kinds of buildings, businesses, and homes might be a part of this drawing?
	Remember, this is not a town in "today" but one that existed in the middle of the last century—about 1950. [They brainstorm]

Unroll a sheet of paper long enough for the entire class to each have drawing space. The paper needs to have the river run through it so that the presence of the river is felt as an integral part of their town and their lives. Students sit on either side of the paper.

Students draw the town. As the teacher moves around, he or she reinforces the ideas of community, continuity, history, and safety. The teacher reminds students that, at this time just in the middle of the century, there might be a movie house, but not a video store; there might be a dry goods store, but not a shopping mall; there might be a grocer, but not a supermarket.

Once students are under way,

Teacher:	As you are drawing, I'd like you to listen to how one child describes her experiences of the town called Swift River. Her story may prompt other ideas you could use to fill out your picture of the town of Swift River.
Teacher reads from:	*Mama let me go to school all alone* to . . . *dipping our fingers down into the sap and tasting the thin sweetness.*

When the students have almost finished their drawing,

Teacher:	Just another couple of minutes to finish up. If you are already finished, collect up the pens.
	Good. Let's take a walk around our town and see what kind of a town we have created. [Students walk around "the town" to see it as a whole]
	As you are walking, talk to the person next to you about what you see, what you notice, and the places with which you identify.
	Now find three or four other people and sit down as a group.

3. The town motto   *5 minutes*

Grouping:	**Groups of 4–5**
Strategy:	**Captioning**
Administration:	**Caption strips (4-by-36-inch); dark felt pens, 1 per group**
Focus:	**To identify the values of the town**

Teacher:

While we are hanging up our mural, decide together what words are carved into the stone lintel above the doors of the town hall. These words are ones that every member of this community would know as part of their lives.

Write them down on the strip of paper you have been given.

One person from each group, please come and place your group's motto on the mural.

When all the mottoes are in place, read them aloud before continuing.

Teacher:

What do these words say about us, the community of Swift River? [Students hold a brief general discussion]

Note: The presence of the mural on the wall serves as a subtle reference and reminder for the rest of the drama.

4. Special insert: Swift River, the heart of America   *12 minutes*

Grouping:	**Dialogue pairs**
Strategy:	**Interview**
Administration:	**Chairs and/or boxes to create the setting**
Focus:	**To build role**

Teacher:

Find a partner and sit down. Decide who is A and who is B.

As, please stand. You are going to be the people who live in Swift River. You have been chosen to be interviewed by a big city newspaper that wants to do a special story about life in small-town America.

Your town of Swift River is seen as one that best represents the ideals and values of mid-twentieth-century America. You have been selected as someone who has a real sense of all that this town has to offer its people and all that its people have to offer the town.

So, who might be some of those people? Perhaps the pastor, the mill owner, the president of the 4-H club, the scout leader, the oldest inhabitant?

Let them provide suggestions; the ideas above can be used to prompt or extend. We are looking for a range of ages, occupations, volunteers in civic activities, schoolkids, teachers, moms, dads, and so on.

Teacher:

Thank you. As, you may sit down. Bs, please stand. You are journalists on the staff of this big city newspaper.

You have been chosen for your abilities to find the human-interest angles. You know just the right questions to ask to get at the heart of this community. Your stories will be part of a special feature insert in the Sunday supplement, so you will need to consider the pictures that might accompany your story.

What might be some of the questions that would give us a good sense of who these people are and what this town represents? For example: What is your oldest memory of this town? What did you used to do when you were a kid? Are the kids still doing that today? I'm sure you have some other ideas. [Students contribute their ideas]

Other ideas that could be offered if students need support:

- Which holiday festival draws you all together?
- What part of the town holds the richest memories for you?
- What part has the river played in your life?

Note: This kind of preparation (for this activity and for the option that follows) prepares the students in advance, not only in terms of what they need to think about, but in letting them in on what the other person is after. It takes the pressure off "what are we supposed to talk about?" and puts it onto creating the stories.

Option

4a. *Building the questions* *5 minutes*

Grouping:	**Whole group**
Strategy:	**Brainstorming**
Administration:	**Chalkboard and chalk**
Focus:	**To develop questioning skills**

<u>Teacher:</u>   What might be some of the questions that would give us a good sense of who these people are and what this town represents?

See prompts above.

<u>Teacher:</u>   The questions that we ask are going to be important, so we must think about them carefully.

The questions that the students devise remain on the board for reference and prompts for the interview.

<u>Teacher:</u>   Townspeople, you have a great responsibility. Choose where the interview will take place. Will it be in your home? In the park? At the town hall, or at your place of work?

Describe your setting to the journalist before you begin your interview and tell him or her what role you will be taking.

You may want to choose a chair or some boxes to help you both feel more "real." Be sure in setting up your scene that you will not be interfering with another group.

When students seem to be organized,

Teacher:	Decide now which one of you will be entering the scene. Those who are entering move away from your partners.
	Everyone ready? Take a moment to think about what is going to happen and what the importance of this scene is for you.
	Stand by. Begin.

Wait until there is stillness and silence before giving the instruction to begin. Students improvise the interview for no longer than three to five minutes, depending upon the experience and maturity of your students.

5. Circle within a circle   10 *minutes*

Grouping:	**As and Bs**
Strategy:	**Circle within a circle**
Administration:	**Outer circle: chairs**
	Inner circle: on the floor
Focus:	**To hear the same event from another point of view; to reflect in role**

Teacher:	Would the townspeople please join me here in a circle on the floor?
	Journalists, please place your chairs in a circle around us. Don't crowd us but be close enough to listen in to what is being said. Journalists, listen carefully but do not speak.
Teacher in role as townsperson:	Well, I'm wondering how that interview went? It was such an honor to be selected. I was quite nervous to think that we had agreed to undertake this responsibility to speak for everyone. Not all of our neighbors would be willing to do that. Tell me about your interview.

Encourage all students to contribute. Part of the skill involved for the teacher is to weave the responses together. For example, "The doctor was saying that he spoke at length about the history of his family. Did that come up in your conversation, John?" The focus is to deepen the commitment; to build the community by hearing all the ideas and stories through debriefing the experience in role. The conversation lies between you and the student who is speaking; try not to let the conversation become generalized. The setup also lets the outside circle hear how effective their questions/responses were. After everyone has contributed his or her story,

Teacher in role:	Thank you. I'm sure it will be a wonderful edition. I can't wait to read it. I only hope that the story doesn't mean that our town is now going to be seen as "the" place to live. Think of what that would mean to our way of life.

Teacher stays seated but slips out of role.

Teacher:	May I see the journalists now? Townspeople, change places with them. Thank you.

Teacher in role as editor:	Welcome back, everyone. I can't tell you how I've been looking forward to this story meeting. It's such a great idea for a big city paper like ours to promote our outlying communities and their unique ways of life. I know we have a winner here! So. To business. Human-interest stories first, I think. Where will we start?

Some prompts may be useful:

- How would you describe the people of Swift River?
- What are some of the adjectives we could use to help our headline writers?
- What interesting highlights did you hear?
- What were some of the photos that we could use to attract readers' interest?

After everyone has contributed,

Teacher in role:	Thank you, ladies and gentlemen. I know this can be an award-winning feature for our paper. It's so important to capture these stories before they disappear.
Teacher:	Just go back to your interview partner and talk for a moment about what you heard. [They do]

This reflection is important because students need a chance to talk to each other about what they have heard and to integrate the experience.

6. Receiving the letter   3 minutes

Grouping:	**Pairs**
Strategy:	**Narration**
Administration:	**Copies of the letter (see Figure 11.1) in individual envelopes, one for each student, labeled "To the Householder"**
Focus:	**To pose the problem**
Teacher:	Find a partner and sit back to back, then close your eyes and just listen.

As the teacher narrates, he or she moves around the class, placing a letter in front of each student.

Teacher narrates:	The people of Swift River were feeling pretty good about themselves and about their town. When they read the Sunday supplement they were proud of each other and of their community. Two months later, without any warning, they received a letter from the state legislature.
Teacher:	Open your eyes now and read the letter you will find on the floor beside you.

Teacher reads the letter aloud as the students read along silently.

The Commissioner
State Water Board
State Legislature

Dear Swift River Householder:

As you may know, discussions have been under way regarding the problem of a diminishing water supply to our cities. We understand that your town is well situated on an excellent source of good, clean, clear, cold water running between the low hills of your valley. Such a resource will provide an excellent site for a new reservoir.

The drowning of your town will make available the millions of gallons of water that will enable our cities and industries to thrive. In the final session of our legislature, your congressmen voted unanimously to flood the towns and valley of Swift River, beginning next spring. We know that this decision will result in a better life for all the citizens of our state.

Our legislature is prepared to offer many different kinds of generous compensation for the inconveniences that may result from our decision. This will enable you to relocate with comfort and with as little disruption to your lives as may be expected under these circumstances.

Although we recognize that your initial response may be negative, we know that after careful thought and consideration, you will see this solution as one that will result in a positive change for everyone concerned.

Our office will be in touch with you in the next few weeks with the details of clearing the land, schedules for the demolition of buildings, relocation of burying grounds and so on.

With every good wish,

Tom C. Banks
Commissioner, State Water Board

cc/   The Mayor
      Municipal Officers

FIGURE 11.1   "To the Householder" Letter

May be photocopied for classroom use. © 2004 *Into the Story Through Drama* by Carole Miller and Juliana Saxton. Heinemann: Portsmouth, NH.

7. The letter-writing campaign

5 minutes

Grouping:	**As in Activity 6**
Strategy:	**Writing in role**
Administration:	**Letter campaign forms (see Figure 11.2) and pencils**
Focus:	**To make our voices heard**

Teacher narrates:

Everyone who read the letter was shocked. How could this happen to them? Although this appeared to be the final word, no one was prepared to accept it.

The people started a letter-writing campaign through which to make their voices heard.

Teacher:

Turn back to your partner and begin to compose what you will say. I will give each pair a letter campaign form and pencil. You will write what you feel would convince the State Legislature Water Board to change its mind.

Please be sure to sign your names. All forms will be witnessed later. [Students write for about five minutes]

Finish up what you are writing. Be sure to sign your name. I will begin to collect the letters.

As the teacher collects the letters, he or she expresses words of encouragement. Some examples:

- Let's hope this works.
- They'll have to listen.
- They can't do this, surely?
- I know how important our voices are.
- They just did a whole newspaper feature on us.
- We are taxpayers, after all.

Option

7a. The petition

10 minutes

Grouping:	**Whole group**
Strategies:	**Writing in role; teacher in role**
Administration:	**Chart paper and black felt pen**
Focus:	**To elevate written language**

In this option, students work together as a community to write the formal petition that will accompany the letters.

Teacher in role
as mayor:

I want to thank all of you citizens of Swift River for your wonderful letters and to thank you for coming to yet another meeting. I am asking for your help to create a formal statement in the form of a petition to accompany our letters of protest.

It is important that the state recognizes the strength and unity of our community of Swift River.

Mr. Banks
The Commissioner
State Water Board
New England State Legislature

Dear Mr. Banks:

Respectfully submitted,

_____

Signature

_____

Date

FIGURE 11.2   Campaign Form Letter

How can we get our government to pay attention to our letters? To sit up and take notice? Governments get these letters all the time, but we know our concerns are critical and they must listen!

How will we word this preamble, this statement of concern?

I thought we might start our petition with something like, "We, the citizens of Swift River . . ."

Teacher in role facilitates the writing of a short, powerful statement of elevated language that synthesizes the concerns of the community. It can be drafted on chart paper or on the board. Outside of class, the teacher formalizes the petition on appropriate paper and with appropriate writing (hand or computer font). During the next class, the petition is signed by all members of the community.

8. The great reservoir rises   3 minutes

Grouping:	**Whole group with individuals in his/her own space**
Strategies:	**Narration; reading aloud (teacher)**
Administration:	**The storybook**
Focus:	**To put in place the historical marker around which to build the end of the story**

Teacher narrates:	In spite of all of these efforts and after many, many meetings, a great deal of bad will, and a great deal of good will on everyone's part, the legislature confirmed its vote "to drown our town [and the others in the valley] that the people in the city might drink."
	As part of the negotiations, the State Historical Board agreed to set aside a piece of land overlooking the new reservoir, and to build a commemorative marker. This marker would be dedicated to the people of Swift River to remind all who visited the reservoir of their sacrifice for the greater good of the greater community.
Teacher reads from:	*First we moved the graves to . . . it took seven long years.*

9. The future   10 minutes

Grouping:	**Groups of 4–5**
Strategies:	**Tableau; captioning**
Administration:	**Paper or card for caption; pencils**
Focus:	**To see the consequences of the event**

Teacher:	Let's have a look at what happened to some of those people who left the town of Swift River and went on to build new lives. In groups of four to five, you will become members of a family. You will give us a glimpse of a moment in your new lives today.
	Remember, it is seven years later—children grow up, new jobs are found, new opportunities appear. For some, life may not be as good as it was; for others the move has given them opportunities they would never have dreamed of in Swift River.

You have two or three minutes to create with your bodies the photograph that you will enclose in a letter to old Swift River friends to catch them up on your life today.

Choose one member of your group to give us a one-sentence description of the photo, something you might write on the back of the picture. For example, "Just finished my first year of teaching. These are the best kids!"

When the students have their tableaux and captions prepared, arrange groups in a circle so that we can move from picture and caption right around the circle without discussion.

Teacher:
When it is your group's turn, I will tell the others to close their eyes while you get ready. We will hear the caption first before I tell everyone to open their eyes.

We won't stop to talk about these, so watch and listen carefully to see how, seven years later, life has changed for the people of Swift River.

Each tableau is shown and the teacher, because there will be no reflection on this activity, needs to make a short reflective comment on the work at the end of the sharing. For example, "Those were very powerful glimpses into your lives. Those photos spoke volumes to us all."

Sometimes the students will want to see one or more tableaux again to clarify their understanding. The students or you may want to have a brief discussion about the tableaux for clarification or because you feel you need to talk a little about coping with change. Or, you may feel that all are ready to move on.

Teacher:
We are moving toward the end of our story and in order to do that, we must return to where it all began.

10. *Reflections at the dedication*   *2 minutes*

Grouping:	**Whole group**
Strategies:	**Narration; reading aloud (teacher)**
Administration:	**The text as adapted**
Focus:	**To identify the story with their own stories**

Teacher narrates:
On the tenth anniversary of the flooding of the valley, the dedication of the historical marker took place.

Many members of the community returned for the ceremony. They were delighted to see each other and to catch up on lost years, to recognize changed faces and to reflect on changed lives.

As the memories flooded back, each one found a place on the hillside overlooking the great reservoir, for their own silent remembering.

Teacher:
Imagine that you are one of those who have returned for the dedication. Find your own place on the hill overlooking the great lake that now fills the valley and see it in your mind's eye. You may want to sit or you may prefer to stand.

Teacher reads:	*That's where the road to Prescott ran,*
	there's the road to Beaver Brook,
	that's the spot the church stood
	where I was baptized.
	And the school.
	And the Grange Hall.
	And the Old Stone Mill.
	We won't be seeing those again.
	I look.
	I think I can see the faint outlines,
	but I can't read the past.
	Little perch now own those streets,
	and bass swim over the country roads.

Note: Because the students are in role and therefore in the "dramatic present," the text is slightly altered to agree with "now" time.

11. Memories   10 *minutes*

Grouping:	**Individuals**
Strategies:	**Voice collage; tapping in; reading aloud (teacher)**
Administration:	**The storybook**
Focus:	**To deepen the drama for internalization**

Teacher:	As you look into the deep water, your own memories begin to rise. Close your eyes and see those memories.
	Choose one that reminds you of something special about your life in Swift River.
	When you feel my hand on your shoulder, just speak that memory aloud. You might want to begin with, "I remember when . . ." or "I shall never forget . . ." and then follow it with your memory.
	After you have spoken your memory, bow your head so that I know you have spoken. Listen to the memories as they flood back, surfacing in the voices of your neighbors and your friends.

Teacher moves around the class, putting a hand on the shoulder of each student until all have spoken. Leave a silence.

| Teacher: | Think about what you have just heard as you listen to the end of our story. |
| Teacher reads from: | *When it got dark . . .* to *. . . winking on and off like fireflies.* |

Omit the following sentence and continue with,

For a moment, I remembered . . . to the end.

Leave a silence—a space for reflection.

12. Processing the experience   5 minutes

Grouping:	**Individuals**
Strategies:	**Writing in role; drawing**
Administration:	**Paper, crayons, felts, etc.**
Focus:	**To reflect individually**

Teacher distributes materials.

Teacher: We've been on quite a long journey together and you have many thoughts and feelings about that journey. For some of you those thoughts will come as words; for others, as pictures.

                                      When you are ready, just write or draw what is in your mind.

Give students about three to five minutes to reflect through writing or drawing or both.

13. Making connections between the story and our lives   10 minutes

Grouping:	**Pairs or groups of 3; whole group**
Strategy:	**Discussion**
Administration:	**None**
Focus:	**To reflect together on the whole experience**

Teacher: Turn to the person next to you and talk about your experience in the drama today. You may, if you wish, share your work. [Students share for a few minutes]

Teacher: I wonder if anyone has something to share with us all?

This initial debriefing will generally be about personal experience and personal revelations. To help debrief the experience on a more universal level and to assess the new meanings, you will want to refer to your key questions and understandings as guides. For example:

- What does this story tell us about how people cope with the challenges of change?
- What does the story tell us about the role that memory plays in giving us strength?
- What is it about people that makes a community?

You might want to make students aware of current events.

"On June 1, 2003, after ten years of construction, authorities closed the sluice gates of the Three Gorges Dam [in China]. . . . The water will overrun the remains of 13 cities, 140 towns and 1352 villages, all destroyed for the promise of hydro power" (*Maclean's*, June 16, 2003, p. 13).

Resources

Dickinson, P. 1965. "The Dam." In *Poets of Our Time: An Anthology*, edited by F. Finn. (p. 41). London: J. Murray.

Kurtz, J. 2000. *River Friendly, River Wide*. New York: Simon & Schuster.

Yolen, J. 1992. *Letting Swift River Go*. Boston: Little, Brown & Co.

Materials

We assume that you will have a chalkboard and chalk available, and a copy of the story, with stickies to mark the parts to be read aloud.

Activity 1:	Overhead: The first illustration in the text
Activity 2:	Long roll of paper with drawing of the river through the length of it; pastels/crayons/felts, masking tape
Activity 3:	Caption strips (4-by-36-inch) dark felt markers (1 per group)
Activities 4, 5:	Chairs
Activity 6:	Copy of letter (Fig. 11.1) in an envelope addressed "To the Householder" for each student
Activity 7:	Campaign form letter (Fig. 11.2) and pencils
Activity 7a:	Chart paper, dark felt pen
Activity 9:	Paper or index cards for photo caption, pencils
Activity 12:	Paper, crayons, felts, pencils

Recommended Reading

Ackroyd, J., ed. 2000. *Literacy Alive! Drama and Literacy Projects*. London: Hodder & Stoughton.

Ackroyd, J., and J. Boulton. 2001. *Drama Lessons for Five to Eleven Year Olds*. London: David Fulton.

Booth, D. 1994. *Story Drama: Reading, Writing and Roleplaying Across the Curriculum*. Markham, ON: Pembroke.

Booth, D., and B. Barton. 2000. *Story Works: How Teachers Can Use Shared Stories in the New Curriculum*. Markham, ON: Pembroke.

Brown, V., and S. Pleydell. 1999. *The Dramatic Difference*. Portsmouth, NH: Heinemann.

Burke, M., and C. Malczewski. 1988. *Social Studies Through Drama*. Victoria, BC: Learning Through Drama.

Clark, J., W. Dobson, T. Goode, and J. Neelands. 1997. *Lessons for the Living*. Toronto, ON: Mayfair Cornerstone.

Cusworth, R., and J. Simons. 1997. *Beyond the Script*. Sydney, NSW: Primary English Teaching Association of Australia.

Davies, G. 1988. *Practical Primary Drama*. Portsmouth, NH: Heinemann.

Grady, S. 2000. *Drama and Diversity: A Pluralistic Perspective for Educational Drama*. Portsmouth, NH: Heinemann.

Heinig, R. B. 1992. *Improvisation with Favorite Tales*. Portsmouth, NH: Heinemann.

Kempe, A., ed. 1996. *Drama Education and Special Needs*. Cheltenham, UK: Stanley Thornes.

Lundy, K. (project coordinator). 1997. *The Treasure Chest: Story, Drama and Dance/Movement in the Classroom*. Toronto, ON: Toronto Board of Education.

Manley, A., and C. O'Neill. 1997. *Dreamseekers: Creative Approaches to the African American Heritage*. Portsmouth, NH: Heinemann.

Morgan, N., and J. Saxton. 1987. *Teaching Drama: A Mind of Many Wonders*. Cheltenham, UK: Stanley Thornes.

———. 1995. *Asking Better Questions*. Markham, ON: Pembroke.

Neelands, J. 1990. *Structuring Drama Work*. London: Cambridge Press.

———. 1998. *Beginning Drama 11–14*. London: David Fulton.

O'Neill, C., and A. Lambert. 1976. *Drama Guidelines*. Oxford, UK: Heinemann Educational Books.

O'Neill, C., A. Lambert, R. Linnell, and J. Warr-Wood. 1982. *Drama Guidelines*. Oxford, UK: Heinemann.

O'Toole, J., and J. Dunn. 2002. *Pretending to Learn: Helping Children Learn Through Drama*. Frenchs Forest, NSW: Pearson Education Australia.

Saldana, J. 1995. *Drama of Color: Improvisation with Multiethnic Folklore*. Portsmouth, NH: Heinemann.

Swartz, L. 2002. *The New Drama Themes*. 3d ed. Markham, ON: Pembroke.

Smith, J., and J. Herring. 2001. *Dramatic Literacy: Using Drama and Literature to Teach Middle Level Content*. Portsmouth, NH: Heinemann.

Tarlington, C., and P. Verriour. 1991. *Role Drama*. Markham, ON: Pembroke.

Warren, K. 1992. *Hooked on Drama*. Sydney, NSW: MacQuarie University Press.

Winston, J. 2000. *Drama, Literacy and Moral Education 5–11*. London: David Fulton.

Winston, J., and M. Tandy. 1998. *Beginning Drama 4–11*. London: David Fulton.

Woolland, B. 1993. *The Teaching of Drama in the Primary School*. London: Longman.

Bibliography

Ackroyd, J., ed. 2000. *Literacy Alive! Drama Projects for Literacy Learning.* London: Hodder and Stoughton.

Baldwin, P. 1998. "Drama and Literacy." *Drama* 5 (3): 15–18.

Barone, T. 1998. "Aesthetic Dimensions of Educational Supervision." In *Handbook of Research on School Supervision,* edited by G. Firth & E. Pajak (pp. 1104–22). New York: Macmillan Publishing Co.

Bateson, M. C. 1994. *Peripheral Visions: Learning Along the Way.* New York: HarperCollins.

Booth, D. 1994. *Story Drama: Reading, Writing and Roleplaying Across the Curriculum.* Markham, ON: Pembroke.

Booth, D., and B. Barton. 2000. *Story Works: How Teachers Can Use Shared Stories in the New Curriculum.* Markham, ON: Pembroke.

Booth, D., and K. Reczuch. 1996. *The Dust Bowl.* Toronto, ON: Kids Can Press.

Booth, E. 1999. *The Everyday Work of Art: Awakening the Extraordinary in Your Daily Life.* Naperville, IL: Sourcebooks, Inc.

Boulton, J. 1997. *Only Opal: The Diary of a Young Girl.* New York: Putnam & Grosset Group.

———. 1995. *Opal: The Journal of an Understanding Heart.* New York: Random House, Three Rivers Press.

———. 1976. *Opal.* New York: Macmillan.

Bradburne, E. S., and O. Whiteley. 1962. *Opal Whiteley, The Unsolved Mystery, together with Opal Whiteley's Diary, The Journal of an Understanding Heart.* London: Putnam.

British Columbia Ministry of Education, Skills and Training. 1998. *Fine Arts Kindergarten to Grade 7: Integrated Resource Package.* Victoria, BC:

Ministry of Education, Skills and Training, Province of British Columbia.

Browne, A. 1992. *The Tunnel*. London: Walker Books Ltd.

Champions of Change: The Impact of the Arts on Learning. 1998. NEA Partnerships in Arts Education and the Kennedy Center. Washington, DC.

Cusworth, R., and J. Simons. 1997. *Beyond the Script*. Sydney, NSW: Primary English Teaching Association of Australia.

Damasio, A. 1994. *Descarte's Error: Emotion, Reason, and the Human Brain*. New York: Putnam.

———. 1999. *The Feeling of What Happens: Body and Emotion in the Making of Consciousness*. New York: Harcourt.

Deasy, R., ed. 2002. *Critical Links: Learning in the Arts and Student Academic and Social Development*. Washington, DC: Arts Education Partnership.

Estes, T., and D. Vásquez-Levy. 2001. "Literature as a Source of Information and Values." *Phi Delta Kappan* (March): 507–12.

Gardner, H. 1983. *Frames of Mind: The Theory of Multiple Intelligences*. New York: Basic Books.

Haseman, B. 2003. Course Outline for Summer Drama Institute. University of Victoria, July.

Heathcote, D., and G. Bolton. 1995. *Drama for Learning: Dorothy Heathcote's Mantle of the Expert Approach to Education*. Portsmouth, NH: Heinemann.

Holden, J. 1994. "Fear of Flying." *Broadsheet: The Journal for Drama in Education* 10 (3): 2–12.

Kempe, A. 1997. "Into the Woods: Animating Stories Through Drama." Unpublished Paper. Reading, UK: University of Reading.

Lee, O., and S. Fradd. 1998. "Science for All: Including Students from Non-English Language Backgrounds." *Educational Researcher* 27 (4): 12–20.

Lemieux, M. 1991. *Peter and the Wolf*. Toronto, ON: Kids Can Press.

McGugan, J. 1995. *Josepha: a prairie boy's story*. Calgary, AB: Northern Lights Red Deer College Press.

Miller, T. 1998. "The Place of Picture Books in Middle Level Classrooms." *Journal of Adolescent and Adult Literacy* 41 (5): 376–82.

Moffett, J. 1968. *A Student-Centered Language Arts Curriculum, K–13: A Handbook for Teachers*. Boston: Houghton Mifflin.

Morgan, N., and J. Saxton. 1987. *Teaching Drama: A Mind of Many Wonders*. Cheltenham, UK: Stanley Thornes.

———. 1994. *Asking Better Questions*. Markham, ON: Pembroke.

———. 1998. "Influences Around the Word." Keynote address read at Ohio Drama Education Exchange Conference, 5–7 June. Columbus, Ohio.

Neelands, J. 1984. *Making Sense of Drama*. London: Heinemann.

———. 1990. *Structuring Drama Work*. London: Cambridge Press.

———. 2000. "Live Language." In *Literacy Alive! Drama Projects for Literacy Learning*, edited by J. Ackroyd, v–vi. Abingdon, UK: Hodder & Stoughton.

O'Mara, J. 2001. Personal communication. 19 July.

O'Neill, C. 1991. "Artists and Models: Theatre Teachers for the Future." *Design for Arts in Education* 92 (4): 23–27.

———. 1995. *Drama Worlds: A Framework for Process Drama*. Portsmouth, NH: Heinemann.

Opie, I., and P. Opie. 1969. *Children's Games in Street and Playground*. London: Oxford University Press.

O'Toole, J., and J. Dunn. 2002. *Pretending to Learn: Helping Children Learn Through Drama*. Frenchs Forest, NSW: Pearson Education Australia.

Raths, J., J. Pancella, and J. Van Ness, eds. 1971. *Studying Teaching*. Englewood Cliffs, NJ: Prentice-Hall.

Sautter, R. 1994. "An Arts Education School Reform Strategy." *Phi Delta Kappan* (February): 432–37.

Taylor, P. 2000. *The Drama Classroom: Action, Reflection, Transformation*. London: Routledge Falmer.

Van Allsburg, C. 1985. *The Polar Express*. New York: Houghton Mifflin.

Wagner, B. J., ed. 1998. *Educational Drama and Language Arts: What Research Shows*. Portsmouth, NH: Heinemann.

———. 1999. rev. ed. *Dorothy Heathcote: Drama as a Learning Medium*. Portland, ME: Calender Islands.

Wagner, J., and R. Roennfeldt. 1995. *The Werewolf Knight*. Sydney, NSW: Random House.

Warner, C. 1997. "The Edging in of Engagement: Exploring the Nature of Engagement in Drama." *Research in Drama Education* 2 (1): 21–42.

Wild, M., and J. Bevis. 1990. *The Very Best of Friends*. Orlando, FL: Harcourt Brace and Company.

Yolen, J. 1992. *Letting Swift River Go*. Boston: Little, Brown & Co.

Zagwÿn, D. T. 1995. *The Pumpkin Blanket*. Markham, ON: Fitzhenry & Whiteside.

Glossary of Drama Strategies

There are a number of strategies listed in the story drama structures that are familiar to all teachers: brainstorming, listening, designing, discussion, drawing, mapping, movement, planning, predicting, puzzles, reading aloud, silent follow-along, and storytelling. Although some appear in the structures, we do not list them. The following strategies have a particular or significant use for the story drama structures.

We have tried to clarify the explanation of each strategy through the teacher talk in the structures. However, when a strategy is new to the group, it may need to be explained in more detail, demonstrated or practiced. As the strategies become more familiar, the students may need only a reminder of what the terms mean.

building an image A participant or the teacher acts as a blank canvas upon which the rest of the group can "draw" their ideas. Participants respond to the invitation to create the image by physically adjusting the body of another person as if it were "clay." The teacher or participant may ask questions; for example, "Is this how you want me to hold my arm?" or, "Where should I focus my eyes?" This is an excellent way to discover what participants are thinking about the person that they are going to meet in role. It also prepares the facilitator for what may come.

building lists List building is a useful, nonjudgmental way to discover and share what is in the minds of individuals and the collective understanding of the group.

building questions While information gathering is important, the value of questions is to inquire into thinking, attitudes, and motivations of others. This is a useful strategy to prepare participants for an improvisation or a hot seating activity. Participants learn to ask and answer open-ended questions.

captioning Captioning expresses meaning in written form through a succinct statement that underscores what is being presented visually. Captioning may also be referred to as headlines or titles.

circle within a circle   This strategy usually follows a pair improvisation or interview. It is very structured in that the teacher in role
has control of the proceedings; all the conversation is directed
through him or her. Two groups, the As and Bs, form two circles
one inside the other. The teacher joins the inside circle to debrief
or reflect on the conversation that has just taken place in the improvisation from the point of view of the inner circle. The role the
teacher takes is congruent with the interests of the people in the
inner circle. The role may not have been seen before. For example,
the editor of the newspaper talks to the reporters. The outside
circle has an opportunity to eavesdrop on the discussion and to
hear how their partners perceived the event. The outside circle
must not comment or interject. They will have their turn when the
circles are reversed. You may choose to have the pairs meet out of
role to talk about what they have just heard.

conscience alley   Participants form two lines facing each other and
the person who has made or must make a decision walks slowly
between. As he or she moves down the line, the pair on either side
of the person comment or reflect (either as themselves or in role)
on the difficulty or choice. The lines act as a collective conscience
and they may give the character advice based on moral or political
choices. Another use for conscience alley is to express the thinking
or feeling of the character who is moving down the line.

dramatic play   Participants are involved in make-believe situations
that do not necessarily require them to be anyone other than
themselves. Dramatic play enables participants to explore reac-
tions and actions in a spontaneous way while at the same time,
constraining their language and behavior to conform to the make-
believe situation.

found poetry   Found poetry is created by using the words and images in a text to create a new text that layers in the participants'
own thoughts and feelings.

games   Games develop group skills and help participants to discover
how rules make things work; they are useful diagnostic devices
for assessing group health. In these story drama structures, we
use games as metaphors or symbolic ways to frame the story. Iona
and Peter Opie in *Children's Games in Street and Playground* (1969)
remind us that all games are analogies for human situations.

gossip mill   Participants are asked to think about one reason that
caused a situation or to share a memory of an event. On a signal
from the teacher, they mill about stopping on a signal to share their
information with another participant. This may be done a number
of times so that the rumors flow. Older students may not need the
signal and can mill about with less structure. The gossip should be
shared, valued, or discounted with the entire group in reflection.

hot seating   Hot seating is used when participants have a need to
expand their understanding by questioning a character in role.
The questions are those that need to be asked and therefore, it is
often useful to prepare at least some in advance. The teacher may
be the person in the hot seat. When using students in hot seating,

it is often safer if they can share the role. This provides opportunities for hearing different perspectives. The purpose is to listen very carefully to each other and build on what is heard and not contradict what has already been said.

improvisation   Improvisation is the basic communicative form for many of the strategies in this glossary. When we improvise, we are moving, thinking, and talking spontaneously, in response to what is happening.

interviewing   Interviews are designed to reveal information, attitudes, motives, and aptitudes of participants in role. Participants, rather than the teacher, are the ones asking questions. The preparation of the questions is an important preliminary activity and can be done collectively, in small groups, pairs, or individually.

mantle of the expert   Participants are endowed with a special expertise in order to accomplish the work. This task-driven activity should be done seriously and with great attention as participants look at the situation through "special" eyes and bring their "expert" understanding and skills into play. It's a wonderful opportunity to elevate students' thinking, language, and presence.

mime   Mime communicates our actions with pretend objects. These actions may be accompanied by words.

narration   Narration is used to link one activity to another and is necessary for coherence. The teacher tells of the events that happened in between activities that will not be experienced by the participants. Narration requires the skills of the storyteller in order to heighten the significance of events and to provide an affective resonance to them.

presentation   The focus of presentation is on the process of making. Presentations are not meant to be valued for their polish, but for what they contribute to understanding.

private instruction   Part of the group will be given information that is not shared with the others. This strategy sets tension simply because it is secret. It is a way to help move the drama forward and to deepen the experience for everyone. It is not about trying to guess the secret instructions.

reading a picture   Participants make meaning from illustrations that introduce them to themes, characters, settings, and the affective context of stories to prepare for the drama. Participants' experiences, knowledge, and values are brought to the reading and are shared collectively through their responses. It is an effective way of introducing the subtleties of signs.

re-enacting   The re-creation of the actions in the text is referred to as re-enactment. Re-enacting can be done as the text is being read or following the reading. During a reading, the participants are able to connect with the affective context as they re-enact. When used following the reading, participants are much more engaged in remembering the sequence of events. In both, there is an emphasis on accuracy of detail and making the drama real.

reflection   Reflection helps the participant stand back from the drama and to consolidate the meanings and/or issues that are emerging.

Reflection is also a means of reviewing and commenting on the action. Reflection not only happens at the end of the drama experience as a way of moving away from the fictional world, but it also occurs both in role and out of role. There are many strategies that encourage reflection because it is a significant means by which participants may bring their own thoughts and feelings into their understanding of the drama, themselves, and others.

retelling   Participants are asked to retell the events through the eyes of other characters in the story. This encourages considering multiple perspectives.

ritual   This strategy slows down and elevates the significance of the action; for example, the signing of a petition. It is a powerful means for moving participants more deeply into the drama because it enables them to recognize the importance of their actions.

role   Working in role is foundational to drama. It is the means by which participants enter into the world of pretend, something that all children can do very well. To be in role means to assume the attitudes and points of view of a fictitious person. The skills demanded by role-playing are simply those of thinking "as if I were walking in someone else's shoes." The only rule for role-playing is that what is said and done in role must be true to the context of the character. When participants are working in role, they are protected by the role and therefore are able to express themselves in ways that may be different from their own.

role on the wall   Life-size blank cutouts or outlines drawn on the board may be used to build background by having participants write words or phrases that describe the character and/or thoughts and feelings of the character. These figures may be returned to and/or words added as a means of reflecting new understanding.

sculpting (or molding)   As in *building an image*, one person shapes someone (usually a partner) into a figure that represents the sculptor's image or perception of that image. The partner acts as "clay" and responds to the touch or direction of his or her partner. The less talking the better. This strategy involves trust; participants need to be reminded to respect their partners and their ability to be shaped.

soundscape   This is a free-form composition using any arrangement of sounds and any combination of traditional instruments, nontraditional instruments, found objects, voices (words or sounds), and body percussion. It creates a picture in sound of a particular location, mood, or dramatic setting.

tableau (also known as depiction or still picture)   Tableau is a frozen, three-dimensional picture of a person or group of people, representing their understanding of a particular context. Although it may be abstract, it represents concretized thinking. Sometimes it is enough just to see a tableau; sometimes you may want to focus the observations by asking, "What do we see?" or by tapping in: "To whom shall we speak?" "What question shall we ask?" This strategy is useful for developing participants' presentational skills as well as audience skills. It is a powerful way to work in drama but is low-risk for both participants and facilitator.

tapping in Participants are frozen (as in tableau) or sitting or standing still, often with their eyes closed. The teacher moves through the group placing a hand on each participant's shoulder and asking a question such as, "Tell me what you are thinking." "What are your concerns?" Keep your hand, gently but firmly, on the participant's shoulder until you are sure the statement has been completed. Sometimes participants are not prepared to speak; leave your hand in place until this is clear and then move on without comment.

teacher in role The teacher takes part in the drama as a way of monitoring and facilitating the learning from inside the story. Teacher in role enables the shift of responsibility for discovery from the teacher to the participants. It allows the teacher to be in control without being didactic. The role must guide the responses demanded by the role, not by the individual who inhabits it.

teacher in role (fringe) Sometimes teacher in role will take a specific character in the story. Other times, teacher in role is just one of the crowd, not necessarily identifiable, but someone who has the right to be there.

transformation Transformation lies at the heart of theatre. Participants exercise their ability to suspend disbelief. Transformation is used to stimulate the imagination. Participants can transform objects (jacket), people (knights), and places (the classroom into a town hall, a medieval castle). In the role of a character, participants are transformed and the experience of that transformation has the potential for transforming them in the real world.

voice collage Participants speak aloud a phrase or sentence from a piece of writing (in or out of role). The teacher can control the collage by tapping in, or participants may speak aloud as they feel their phrases or sentences fit. The teacher needs to be sensitive as to when the collage is over. Generally, "thank you" indicates that the collage is concluded. Voice collages are often used to create a mood or to let participants hear what other members of the group are thinking.

writing in role This strategy is used as a means of reflecting inside the drama on the experience in the drama. The writing is always purposeful whether it is recording personal thoughts in a diary, appealing to a greater authority through a petition, communicating with a friend or administrator by letter, or making information available through a newspaper article. The context of the drama provides the motivation for all kinds of writing that may be used in a variety of ways in the drama.

For our glossary, we have relied on the work of Morgan and Saxton (1987); Neelands (1990); British Columbia Ministry of Education (1998); and O'Toole and Dunn (2002).

Index